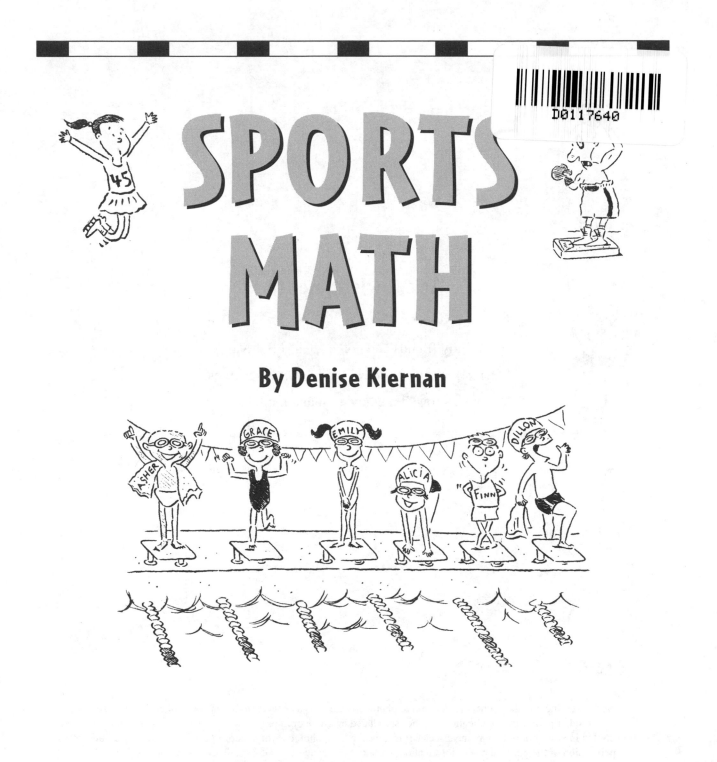

# SPORTS MATH

## By Denise Kiernan

### SCHOLASTIC
### PROFESSIONAL BOOKS

New York • Toronto • London • Auckland • Sydney
Mexico City • New Delhi • Hong Kong

# Acknowledgments

For all my friends and colleagues at Scholastic's
*DynaMath*, *Math Power*, and *Math* magazines,
who showed me how to make math fun.

Cover design by Jaime Lucero
Cover illustration by Mike Moran
Interior design by Sydney Wright
Interior illustrations by Mike Moran

ISBN 0-590-21966-9

# Contents

# Introduction

Welcome to the math workout your students will love!

Kids of all ages are playing and watching sports more now than ever before. For that reason, *Sports Math* was designed to show students that they can find math in the most unlikely of places—even while playing or watching some of their favorite sports.

The activities themselves cover a wide variety of sports and highlight the way math is used in each. Each activity focuses on a different skill so that the book can be used throughout the school year to keep math skills sharp. The Table of Contents lists each activity title and the primary skill that it covers. The activities have also been written with the National Council of Teachers of Mathematics (NCTM) standards in mind. It is important to understand that while *Sports Math* uses some of the language and rules found in the sports that it features, neither the teacher nor the students need to have any knowledge about the sport being featured in the activity.

Each activity features a *For the Teacher* page that will explain the activity in detail, give examples, and explain any rules. The accompanying page is a reproducible that can be photocopied and handed out to students. The easy-to-use activities can stand alone as classroom work, be used to review important math concepts, or be given to students as homework assignments or for extra credit.

Many of the activities also include Extension Activities to help you extend the learning. The activities come in a variety of shapes and sizes and take the technique presented in the activity into the outside world. In many cases, students are encouraged to look around at their school environment and beyond to take the skill they've just worked with and apply it in another setting, which may or many not be sports. The extension activities are often suited to long-term projects and teamwork.

You'll also find All-Star Math questions included with some of the activities. These questions challenge students to apply the math skills they have been working with at a higher level. The All-Star Math questions are ideal for more advanced students to do on their own or for students to work on in small groups.

As you use **Sports Math** in your classroom, we hope you'll find activities that engage and motivate all your students and help them to recognize how they can use their math skills in many ways and many places—from scoring a game of golf to calculating who will win a race!

# Math Anyone?

## Serve up a fun game to help students practice basic math operations.

### Learning Objective

Students play a game to review basic math operations including addition, subtraction, multiplication, and division.

### What You'll Need

paper
pencil
calculator (optional)

### Directions

1. Explain to students that they will be working in groups of three. One student will be the umpire, while the other two are the tennis players.

2. Students decide who will serve first. A student "serves" by posing a whole-number math problem, that has a whole-number answer, to his or her opponent. Problems may be multiplication, division, addition, or subtraction.

3. Students may use pencil and paper to do their calculations. For example: The first student serves with "72 divided by 8." The second student "returns" the serve by first giving the correct answer, 9, and then using that answer in another equation of his or her choosing. So the second student can then say, "Add 4,322 and 9," and the first student has to give the correct answer and use that answer in another problem. The problems given must have whole-number answers.

4. It is the job of the umpire to determine if the answers given are correct and if the question asked has a whole-number answer. If a student serves a problem that does not have a whole-number answer, it is considered a "fault," and the student can try again. If the student again serves an invalid problem, it is considered a "double fault" and the student loses the serve. The opponent continues by serving a problem using the same number. The umpire can use a calculator to check any facts. The umpire can also record all of the problems and keep score on a blank sheet of paper.

5. **To Score the Game:** For every correct answer given, a student gets a point. For every fault, a point is taken away. In the event of a double fault, the student loses two points, and his or her opponent earns one. The first student to score ten points wins.

### Extension Activity

• As the class advances and its skill level progresses, the game can become more complex. Students can challenge each other by incorporating problems that use fractions or decimals. You can also adjust the game to target specific math skills. For example, students who are having difficulty with their multiplication facts might play several rounds of the game using only multiplication problems.

# Dive into Math

## Students plunge the depths of their measurement ability in a cool math pool.

### Learning Objective

Students review metric units of measurement and practice converting meters into feet and inches.

### What You'll Need

Dive into Math reproducible (page 9)
pencil
calculator (optional)

### Directions

1. Distribute the Dive into Math reproducible to the students. Tell students that in this activity, they will be converting meters into feet and inches.

2. Review the metric system with students and explain that the metric system is used regularly in many parts of the world and is used for scientific measurement. Draw students' attention to the conversion chart at the bottom of the reproducible and tell students to use the chart to answer the questions on the page.

3. This is an excellent exercise for calculator practice. Explain to students that after they have made their calculations, they should round their answers to the nearest inch, foot, or meter.

### Extension Activities

• Send students on a metric scavenger hunt. Have them make a list of places where they see the metric system being used. In addition to sporting events, students may find the metric system on food or beverage labels, in their science lab, or on the speedometer of their parents' car.

• Explain to students that in other parts of the world students their own age measure their height in meters. Challenge students to convert their own height in feet and inches to meters.

### Answers

| | |
|---|---|
| 1a. 157 inches | 3. 476 inches |
| 1b. 13 feet | **All-Star Math** |
| 2a. 240 inches | 4. 157 inches |
| 2b. 6 meters | 5. 6¹/₂ feet |

# Dive into Math

Look at the picture and answer the questions. Use the conversion chart at the bottom of the page to compute your answers.

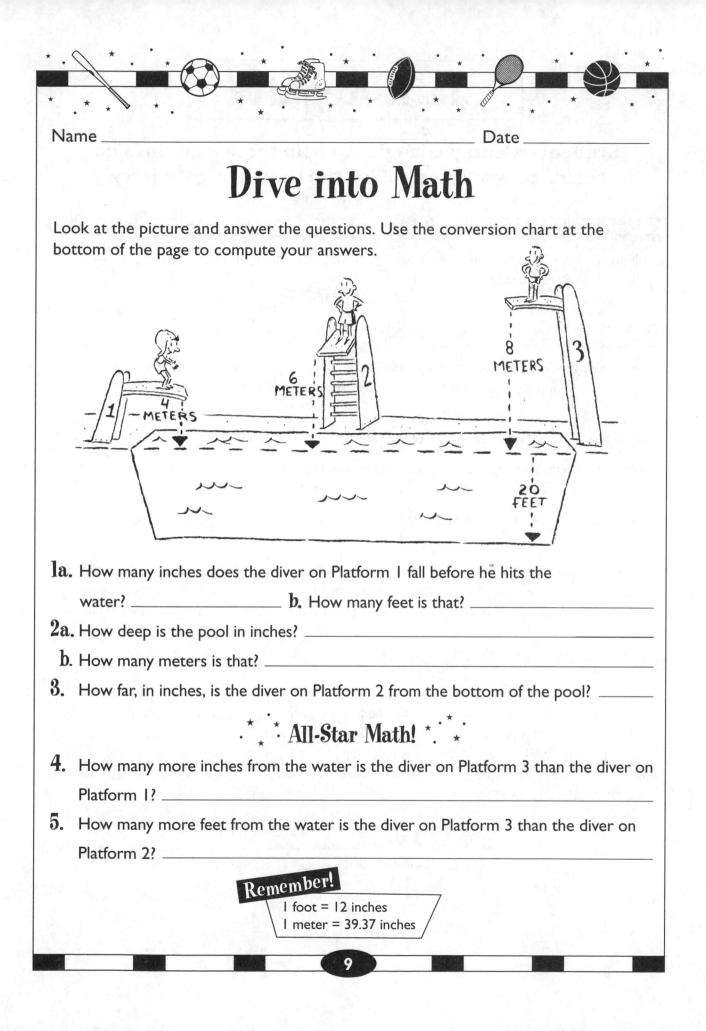

**1a.** How many inches does the diver on Platform 1 fall before he hits the

water? _____ **b.** How many feet is that? _____

**2a.** How deep is the pool in inches? _____

 **b.** How many meters is that? _____

**3.** How far, in inches, is the diver on Platform 2 from the bottom of the pool? _____

## ⋆ ⋆ All-Star Math! ⋆ ⋆

**4.** How many more inches from the water is the diver on Platform 3 than the diver on

Platform 1? _____

**5.** How many more feet from the water is the diver on Platform 3 than the diver on

Platform 2? _____

**Remember!**

1 foot = 12 inches
1 meter = 39.37 inches

# Math Regatta

## Students identify triangles to help these captains find their boats and set sail for the shores of geometry.

### Learning Objective

Students learn to distinguish obtuse, acute, equilateral, and right triangles.

### What You'll Need

Math Regatta reproducible (page 11)
pencil
protractor

### Directions

1. Distribute the Math Regatta reproducible to the class. Explain that in this activity students will have to identify equilateral, acute, obtuse, and right triangles.

2. Review with students the different types of triangles and how they are identified, drawing their attention to "Triangle Tips" at the bottom of the reproducible page.

3. Students should identify the triangle sails on each boat and write the name of that triangle on the sail. They can use a protractor to measure the angles.

4. Once all triangles have been identified, students should draw a line from each sailor to his or her sailboat.

5. As a follow-up, you might discuss the differences between acute angles and acute triangles. You might also discuss with students triangles that fall into more than one category. For example, an equilateral triangle, like an acute triangle, also has three angles under 90 degrees.

### Extension Activity

• Invite students to create their own geometry Math Regatta on a bulletin board. Ask each student to make a sailboat with two triangle sails and a sailor with a flag that names the type of triangles on the boat. Students can use protractors to make the triangles. Post all of the students' sailboats and sailors on a bulletin board. Students can then match all of the sailors to their sailboats. For a simpler bulletin-board display, have students make only the sailboats with triangle sails and ask students to identify them.

### Answers

Sailors and boats should be matched as follows:
1. D          4. A
2. E          5. C
3. B

# Math Regatta

Help these captains find their boats by matching the triangle names on their flags to the sails on their boats. Draw a line from each captain to his or her boat. Read "Triangle Tips" for help.

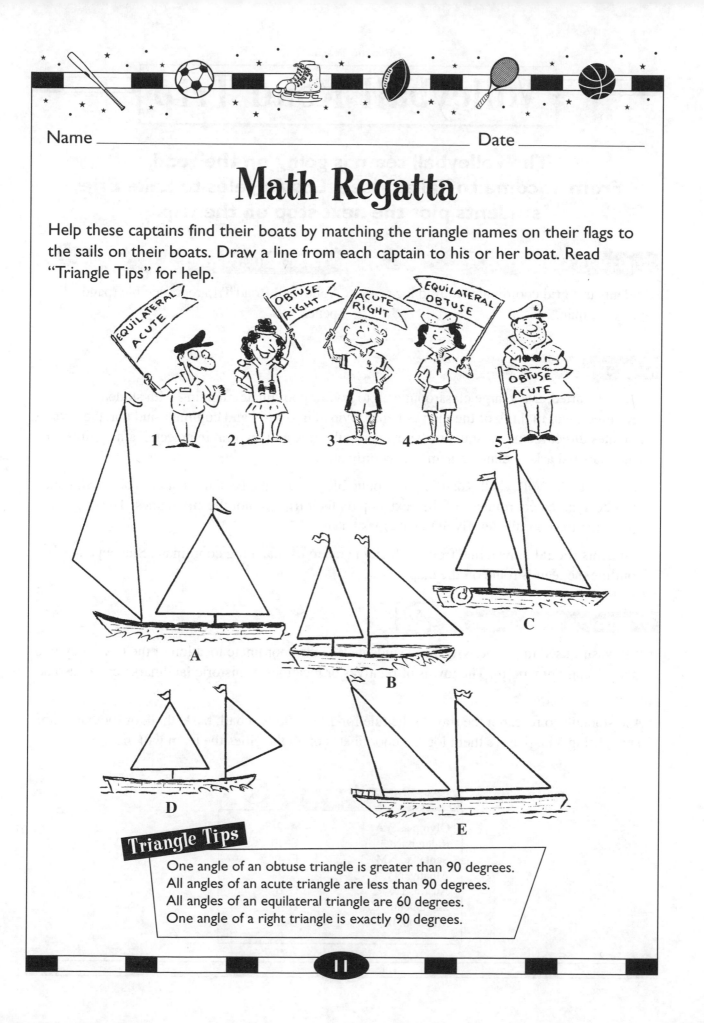

## Triangle Tips

One angle of an obtuse triangle is greater than 90 degrees.
All angles of an acute triangle are less than 90 degrees.
All angles of an equilateral triangle are 60 degrees.
One angle of a right triangle is exactly 90 degrees.

# Volleyball Road Trip

**The volleyball team is going on the road.
From Tacoma to Tallahassee, Los Angeles to Lake Erie,
students plot the next stop on the trip.**

## Learning Objective

Students use grid coordinates to find locations on a map.

## What You'll Need

Volleyball Road Trip reproducible (page 13)
pencil

## Directions

1. To get started, use a large classroom map to review coordinate mapping with students. Remind them to think of the map as being divided into rows and columns, and that the coordinates direct them to a square where a particular row and column intersect. Name points on the map and ask students to name the coordinates.

2. Distribute the Volleyball Road Trip reproducible to students. Explain that the volleyball team has been given coordinates of the next stop on their trip but not the city names. The object is to match the coordinates given to the cities listed.

3. Students should draw a line from each city name to its matching coordinate. Student can then outline the team's route on the map.

## Extension Activities

• If it wasn't used in this activity, have students find the coordinate location of the town they live in as a geography tie-in. The towns of relatives or locations of historic landmarks could also be used.

• Ask students to research the travel schedule for a favorite baseball, basketball, or football team. Then, using a map, have them log the coordinates of all the cities the team will visit.

## Answers

| | |
|---|---|
| Olympia, WA | A–2 |
| Raleigh, NC | E–10 |
| Santa Fe, NM | E–4 |
| Albany, NY | C–11 |
| Austin, TX | G–6 |
| Sacramento, CA | D–1 |
| Madison, IL | C–8 |

# Volleyball Road Trip

Help the volleyball team stay on course! Match each city to its correct map coordinate. Then draw the team's route on the map.

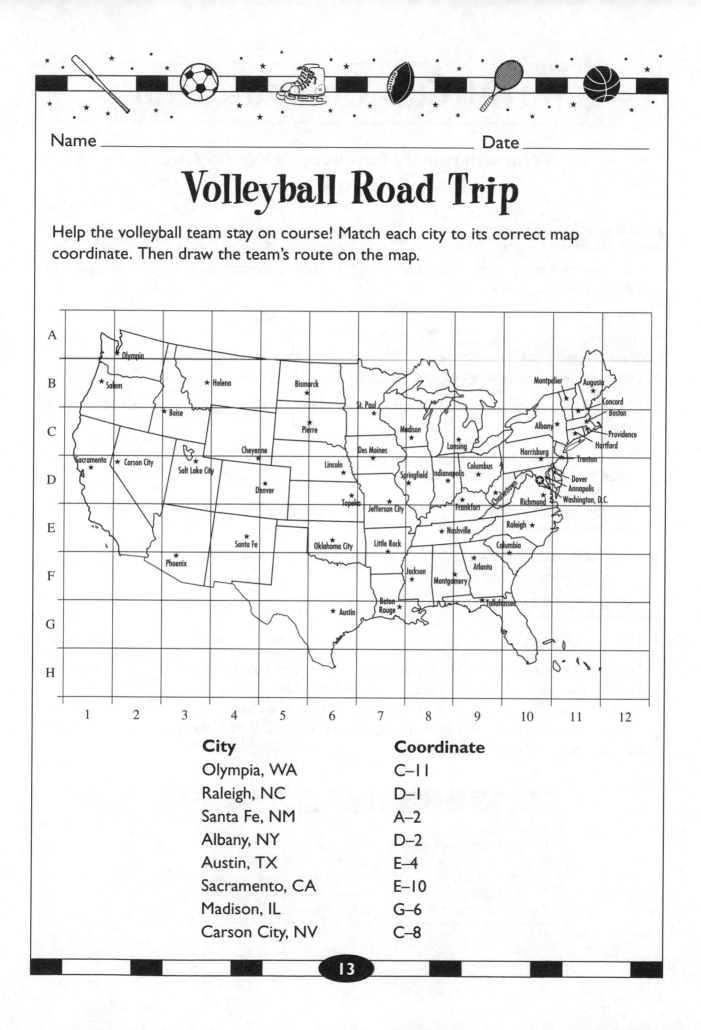

| City | Coordinate |
|------|-----------|
| Olympia, WA | C–11 |
| Raleigh, NC | D–1 |
| Santa Fe, NM | A–2 |
| Albany, NY | D–2 |
| Austin, TX | E–4 |
| Sacramento, CA | E–10 |
| Madison, IL | G–6 |
| Carson City, NV | C–8 |

# World Cup Computation

## Who will qualify for soccer's World Cup?
## Math holds the answer.

### Learning Objective

Students practice computation skills and work with simple equations.

### What You'll Need

World Cup Computation reproducible (page 15)

### Directions

1. Distribute the World Cup Computation reproducible to the class.

2. Review the directions with students. Make sure to go over the number values of win, loss, and draw.

3. Explain to students that they should use multiplication to compute the point values of wins, losses, and draws for each country.

4. Students should then add the point totals for wins, losses, and draws together to arrive at the point total for each country.

5. Students should answer the questions at the bottom of the page.

### Extension Activities

• For a fun geography activity, have students find each of the countries on the classroom globe.

• Challenge a group of students to research the results of the qualifying rounds of the 1998 World Cup and use the results to create new math problems. (These results are available in the *World Almanac*.) They can present the results of the first and final rounds of games in a chart that lists the wins, losses, and draws for each team, and then invite other groups of students to determine the points each team earned.

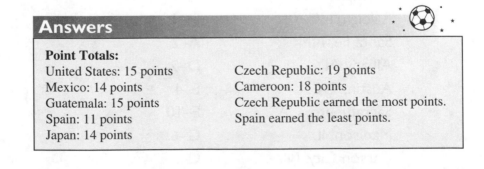

### Answers

**Point Totals:**

United States: 15 points
Mexico: 14 points
Guatemala: 15 points
Spain: 11 points
Japan: 14 points

Czech Republic: 19 points
Cameroon: 18 points
Czech Republic earned the most points.
Spain earned the least points.

Name _____ Date _____

# World Cup Computation

Who will qualify for soccer's World Cup? Math holds the answer!
Add up the points for each of the countries below and write your answers in the blanks.

Example:  2W + 1L + 2D =
          2(3) + 1(0) + 2(1) =
          6 + 0 + 2 = 8 points

| Point Box |
| --- |
| W = Win = 3 points |
| L = Loss = 0 points |
| D = Draw = 1 point |

United States: 4W, 3L, 3D    _____ + _____ + _____ = _____

Mexico: 3W, 2L, 5D    _____ + _____ + _____ = _____

Guatemala: 5W, 5L, 0D    _____ + _____ + _____ = _____

Spain: 3W, 5L, 2D    _____ + _____ + _____ = _____

Japan: 4W, 4L, 2D    _____ + _____ + _____ = _____

Czech Republic: 5W, 1L, 4D    _____ + _____ + _____ = _____

Cameroon: 6W, 4L, 0D    _____ + _____ + _____ = _____

1. Which country earned the most points? _____

2. Which country earned the least? _____

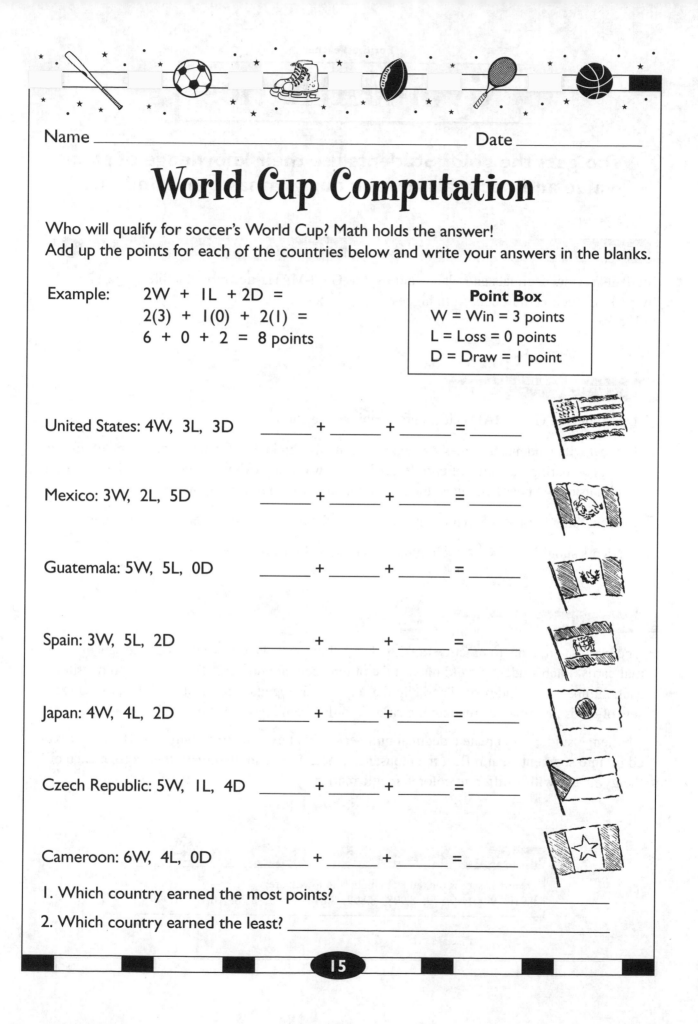

# Gym-MATH-tics

## Who gets the gold? Students use their knowledge of place value and decimals to rank our gymnasts and find out.

### Learning Objective

Students review decimals and place value by ranking decimal numbers from highest to lowest.

### What You'll Need

Gym-MATH-tics reproducible (page 17)
pencil

### Directions

**1.** Distribute the Gym-MATH-tics reproducible to the class.

**2.** Review with students the rules for ranking decimals, reminding them to work from left to right when comparing the value of two decimals. As a warm-up activity, you might write a series of decimals on the board and have the class rank them from highest to lowest.

**3.** Students should rank the gymnasts 1 to 10, with the highest score receiving the number 1.

**4.** Students should then write each gymnast's rank on his or her ribbon.

### Extension Activities

• One way for students to practice ranking decimal numbers is to have them create sets of decimal cards. Each student should make a list of ten decimal numbers. Then they should write each number on an index card and clip the set of cards together. Students can then exchange sets of cards and practice placing the cards in order from highest to lowest.

• Challenge students to create a decimal number line that extends from only 7 to 10 and is divided up into segments that reflect the thousands place. They can then mark the score of each of the gymnasts with a different colored magic marker.

### Answers

Decimals scores ranked from highest to lowest are:
9.910, 9.901, 9.899, 8.998, 8.899, 8.878, 8.877, 8.789, 8.787, 7.999

# Gym-MATH-tics

Who gets the gold? Use your knowledge of place value and decimals to find out.
Rank the decimals from highest to lowest and then fill in the ribbons. Write a "1" on
the ribbon of the gymnast with the highest score, and so on.

8.787

8.878

9.901

9.910

8.998

8.899

9.899

8.877

7.999

8.789

# Math on Track

## It's a race for rate as math helps students find out which driver wins!

### Learning Objective

Students explore the concept of rate as they calculate the time it takes for race car drivers to complete laps around a racetrack.

### What You'll Need

Math on Track reproducible (page 19)
pencil

### Directions

1. Hand out copies of the Math on Track reproducible.

2. Explain to students that in this activity they will be working with rate and time. To begin, review the sample problem with students. Emphasize that when working with time, they should first convert minutes to seconds, do the necessary math, and then convert their answers back to minutes and seconds.

3. To find out how long it takes a driver to complete one lap, students should first convert the time in minutes to seconds. Then they should divide the time elapsed by the number of laps completed. For the final answer, students should convert the time in seconds back to minutes.

### Extension Activities

• As a follow-up, invite students to brainstorm other situations in which they can use this formula. For example, calculating how long it would take a person to travel from New York to Los Angeles traveling at 60 mph or how fast a marathoner will complete a 26-mile race if she has run the first 3 miles in 24 minutes. Students might then write word problems using these situations for other classmates to solve.

• Encourage students to watch a race on television. They can keep track of the time elapsed in a notebook, and make predictions about who will finish first, second, and so on, based on the early performances of the drivers.

### Answers

1. 10 laps
2a. 45 seconds
2b. 18 minutes, 45 seconds
3a. Miles Tuggo is faster at 61 seconds per lap. Slick Vick's rate is 62 seconds per lap.
3b. Slick Vick: 36 minutes, 10 seconds; Miles Tuggo: 35 minutes, 35 seconds
4a. 18 minutes, 38 seconds
4b. 21 minutes, 10 seconds

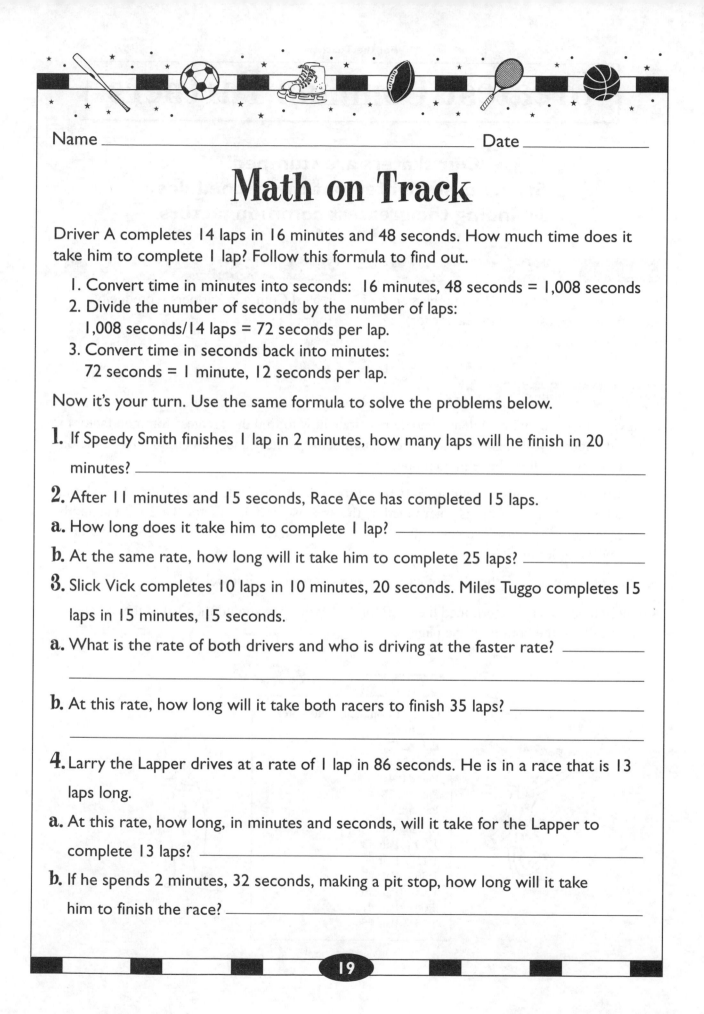

Name _____ Date _____

# Math on Track

Driver A completes 14 laps in 16 minutes and 48 seconds. How much time does it take him to complete 1 lap? Follow this formula to find out.

1. Convert time in minutes into seconds: 16 minutes, 48 seconds = 1,008 seconds
2. Divide the number of seconds by the number of laps:
   1,008 seconds/14 laps = 72 seconds per lap.
3. Convert time in seconds back into minutes:
   72 seconds = 1 minute, 12 seconds per lap.

Now it's your turn. Use the same formula to solve the problems below.

**1.** If Speedy Smith finishes 1 lap in 2 minutes, how many laps will he finish in 20

minutes? _____

**2.** After 11 minutes and 15 seconds, Race Ace has completed 15 laps.

**a.** How long does it take him to complete 1 lap? _____

**b.** At the same rate, how long will it take him to complete 25 laps? _____

**3.** Slick Vick completes 10 laps in 10 minutes, 20 seconds. Miles Tuggo completes 15

laps in 15 minutes, 15 seconds.

**a.** What is the rate of both drivers and who is driving at the faster rate? _____

_____

**b.** At this rate, how long will it take both racers to finish 35 laps? _____

_____

**4.** Larry the Lapper drives at a rate of 1 lap in 86 seconds. He is in a race that is 13

laps long.

**a.** At this rate, how long, in minutes and seconds, will it take for the Lapper to

complete 13 laps? _____

**b.** If he spends 2 minutes, 32 seconds, making a pit stop, how long will it take

him to finish the race? _____

# Greatest Common Partners

## Our skaters are stumped!
## Students straighten out their schedules
## by finding the greatest common factors.

### Learning Objective

Students recognize factors for numbers and identify the greatest common factor for pairs of numbers.

### What You'll Need

Greatest Common Partners reproducible (page 21)
pencil

### Directions

1. Review factoring with students, and demonstrate how to find the greatest common factor of two numbers by listing the factors of each number separately and then circling those factors that the two numbers have in common.

2. Distribute the Greatest Common Partners reproducible to students. Explain that the order in which the skaters perform is determined by the greatest common factor (GCF) of the numbers of each pair of skaters. The pair with the lowest GCF skates first and the others follow in ascending order of GCF.

3. Students should write the GCF of each pair of skaters on the line below them.

4. Once students have determined the GCF for each pair, they should then fill in the "Skater Schedule" at the bottom of the page.

### Answers

Greatest Common Factors are:
Pair #1: 12
Pair #2: 7
Pair #3: 2
Pair #4: 4
Pair #5: 28
Pair #6: 9

Skating Order is:
1:00    Pair #3
1:15    Pair #4
1:30    Pair #2
1:45    Pair #6
2:00    Pair #1
2:15    Pair #5

# Greatest Common Partners

Our skaters have partners but no one knows who's supposed to skate first. The greatest common factors hold the key. Write the greatest common factor (GCF) for each pair of numbers on the line below. Then fill in the Skater Schedule. The pair with the lowest GCF will go first and the others will follow in order from lowest to highest GCF.

1. _____   2. _____   3. _____

4. _____   5. _____   6. _____

**Skater Schedule:**

1:00 _____

1:15 _____

1:30 _____

1:45 _____

2:00 _____

2:15 _____

# Football Frenzy

## The running back just ran 73 yards! How many feet is that? Try this activity to bring students up to speed on measurements.

### Learning Objective

Students reinforce their knowledge of measurement conversions by changing yards into feet, feet into inches, and feet into yards.

### What You'll Need

Football Frenzy reproducible (page 23)
pencil

### Directions

1. Hand out copies of the Football Frenzy reproducible to the class. Tell students that in this activity they will be converting units of measurement.

2. Review measurement conversion with the class. Explain to students that when they are converting from yards to feet, they will be using multiplication. When converting from feet to yards, they will be dividing with a remainder. The remainder is the number of feet left.

### Extension Activity

• Videotape a football game to watch with students during class. While watching a game, you can divide the class into teams and see who can convert yards to feet and/or inches the fastest during the course of the game. Students can convert the length of field goals, passes, punt returns, and more. You may also use football as an opportunity to work on conversion to metric units, encouraging students to convert yards gained by the teams into meters.

### Answers

| | |
|---|---|
| 1a. 66 feet | All-Star Math |
| 1b. 792 inches | 3a. 23 yards, 2 feet |
| 2a. 51 feet | 3b. 17 yards, 1 foot |
| 2b. 117 feet | 3c. 123 feet, 41 yards |
| 2c. 39 yards | 3d. 49 yards, 147 feet |

# Football Frenzy

Our running back just ran 73 yards! How many feet is that?
Answers the questions below by converting the measurements.

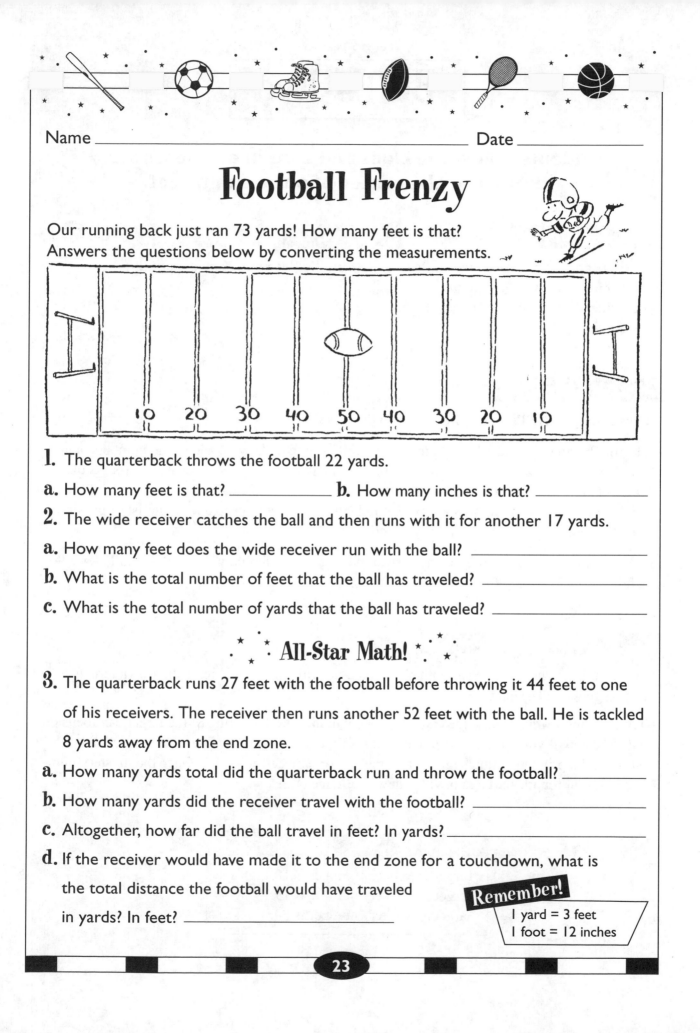

**1.** The quarterback throws the football 22 yards.

**a.** How many feet is that? _____ **b.** How many inches is that? _____

**2.** The wide receiver catches the ball and then runs with it for another 17 yards.

**a.** How many feet does the wide receiver run with the ball? _____

**b.** What is the total number of feet that the ball has traveled? _____

**c.** What is the total number of yards that the ball has traveled? _____

## ⋆ ⋆ All-Star Math! ⋆ ⋆

**3.** The quarterback runs 27 feet with the football before throwing it 44 feet to one
of his receivers. The receiver then runs another 52 feet with the ball. He is tackled
8 yards away from the end zone.

**a.** How many yards total did the quarterback run and throw the football? _____

**b.** How many yards did the receiver travel with the football? _____

**c.** Altogether, how far did the ball travel in feet? In yards? _____

**d.** If the receiver would have made it to the end zone for a touchdown, what is
the total distance the football would have traveled
in yards? In feet? _____

**Remember!**
1 yard = 3 feet
1 foot = 12 inches

# Bull's-Eye

## Students follow the clues and zero in on the mystery number at the center of our math target.

### Learning Objective

Students apply problem-solving skills and review prime numbers, multiples, and dividends as they try to uncover the mystery numbers.

### What You'll Need

Bull's-Eye reproducible (page 25)
pencil

### Directions

**1.** Distribute the Bull's-Eye reproducible to the class.

**2.** Before beginning, make sure students are familiar with odd, even, and prime numbers, and understand the difference between a multiple and a dividend. Also discuss the process of elimination with the class. Emphasize that as they work with each ring, students should be able to narrow down possible answers. Students may wish to keep a running list of possible answers and cross them out as they are eliminated.

**3.** Once they have discovered the mystery number, students should write it in the bull's-eye at the center of the target.

### Extension Activities

• Have students choose a mystery number, come up with clues, and create their own targets to exchange with classmates.

• Try creating a large "challenge" target for the whole class. Each ring of the target can focus on a different skill you have covered in class. Post the target on the wall and invite students to work on the problem at the beginning of the day or between activities. Once the mystery number has been found, start again with a new challenge target.

### Answers

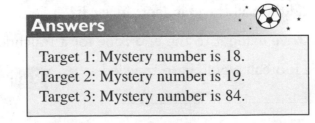

Target 1: Mystery number is 18.
Target 2: Mystery number is 19.
Target 3: Mystery number is 84.

# Bull's-Eye

Follow the clues and zero in on the mystery numbers at the center of our math targets. Read the clues in each ring of our archery targets to find out the mystery number in the bull's-eye. Start with the clues in the outer ring, then work your way to the center.

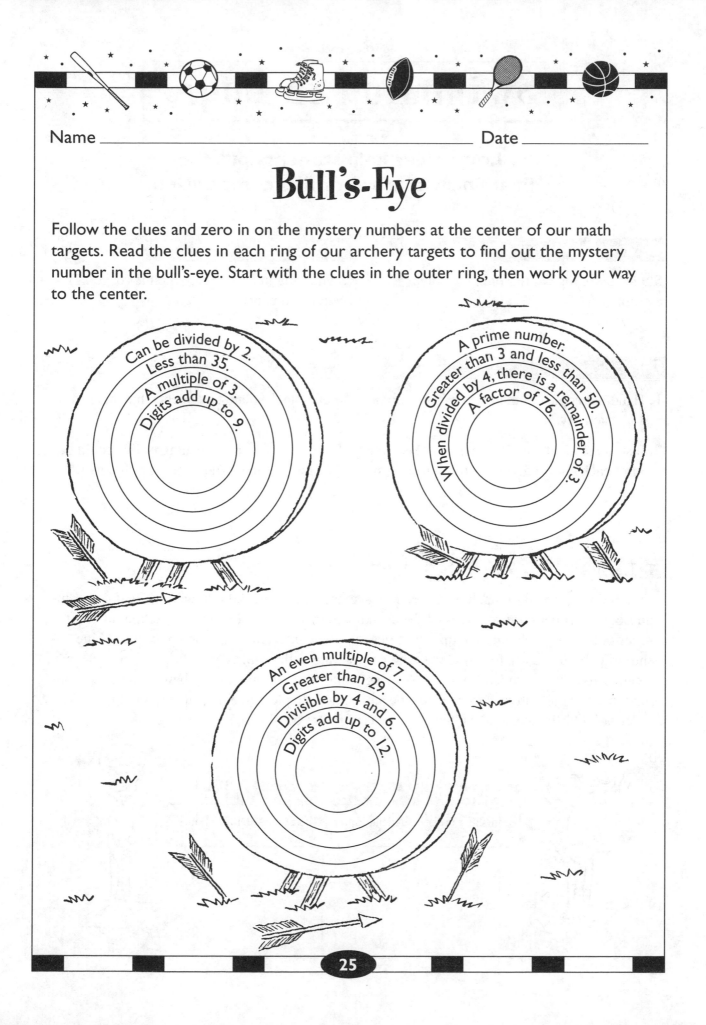

Can be divided by 2.
Less than 35.
A multiple of 3.
Digits add up to 9.

A prime number.
Greater than 3 and less than 50.
When divided by 4, there is a remainder of 3.
A factor of 76.

An even multiple of 7.
Greater than 29.
Divisible by 4 and 6.
Digits add up to 12.

# Swimming in Logic

## Logic clues help students put the final finish on a swimming competition.

### Learning Objective

Students use logical reasoning to solve a problem.

### What You'll Need

Swimming in Logic reproducible (page 27)
pencil and paper

### Directions

**1.** Hand out copies of the Swimming in Logic reproducible. Explain to students that this is a logic activity.

**2.** Instruct students that it is useful to keep track of what the possible finishing orders could be after each clue is given. With each successive clue, the possible order is narrowed down.

### Extension Activity

• Turn lining up to go to lunch or recess into an exercise in logical thinking with a game of Line up Logic. Write a series of clues on the chalkboard that indicate in which order the different groups of students should line up. The clues might include: students who are wearing blue shirts should line up before students who are wearing yellow shirts and after students who are wearing red shirts. Students who are wearing white shirts should line up before students wearing blue. An alternative is to line students up using a simple guideline, such as in alphabetical order or by birth date, and challenge students to figure out the rule you have used.

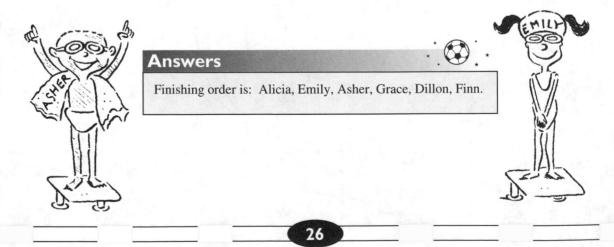

### Answers

Finishing order is: Alicia, Emily, Asher, Grace, Dillon, Finn.

# Swimming in Logic

Logic clues put the final finish on our swimming competition. Read the clues and place these swimmers in the correct finishing order.

### Dive into These Clues!

1. Asher finished before Grace but after Emily.
2. Grace finished after Alicia but before Finn and Dillon.
3. Alicia finished before Emily.
4. Finn came in last.

### Results:

1st _____

2nd _____

3rd _____

4th _____

5th _____

6th _____

# Trade Math

## Students seek out some super stats with America's favorite pastime—math!

### Learning Objective

Students analyze and compare statistics and complete simple computations.

### What You'll Need

Trade Math Cards and Trade Math reproducible (pages 29–30)
pencil

### Directions

1. Hand out copies of the Trade Math Cards and Trade Math reproducibles. Explain to students that they should use the information on the baseball cards to answer the questions on the reproducible. Each baseball card includes the player's birth date, height, weight, hometown, position, and batting average.

2. This activity can be used in conjunction with the following activity, Batting for Decimals.

### Extension Activities

• Arrange several packs of baseball cards on a large sheet of poster board and hang on the classroom wall. Generate a list of questions based on the statistics on the cards and hang next to the poster. Students can answer the questions in their free time. Displaying a large number of cards will make it more of a challenge to find, for example, the tallest player featured.

• Have students make their own cards to be traded in class. The cards can follow the sports model, but can feature any statistical information that the students would like to provide. In addition to basics like birthdays and hometowns, students could include other facts such as their favorite colors or movies, musical instruments played, number of siblings, pets, and more. Encourage them to be as creative as possible. The information can be written on index cards and personalized with a small school picture. Cards can then be then photocopied and "traded" in class. Alternatively, post all of the cards and challenge students to find the answers to questions such as; find five classmates whose birthdays are after yours, find five classmates who are shorter than you; or find the tallest member of the class.

### Answers

| | | |
|---|---|---|
| 1. Ages will vary depending on the year and the time of year. The oldest is Steel N. Home. | 4a. B. Ace Runner | 6b. Shortstop |
| | 4b. Homer Unn | 7a. Sammy Slugger |
| | 5. Steel N. Home | 7b. Portland, Oregon |
| 2. Sammy Slugger | 6a. Izzy Saif | 7c. 183 pounds |
| 3. Sammy Slugger | | |

# Trade Math Cards

**Steel N. Home**
7/31/72    5'11"    187 lbs.
Chicago, IL
Third base    .282

**Izzy Saif**
1/10/74    6'0"    190 lbs.
Nashville, TN
Shortstop    .275

**B. Ace Runner**
11/5/75    6'2"    195 lbs.
Tulsa, OK
Pitcher    .288

**Sammy Slugger**
8/24/76    5'10"    183 lbs.
Portland, OR
Right field    .322

**Homer Unn**
4/8/74    6'1"    200 lbs.
Orlando, FL
Catcher    .313

# Trade Math

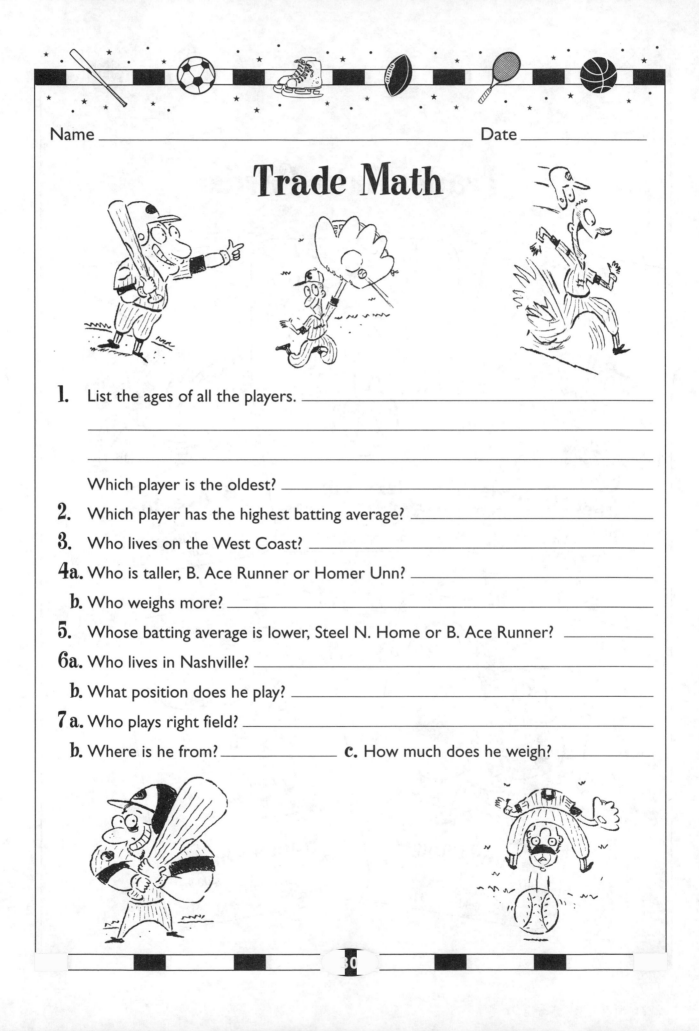

1. List the ages of all the players. _____

_____

_____

   Which player is the oldest? _____

2. Which player has the highest batting average? _____

3. Who lives on the West Coast? _____

4a. Who is taller, B. Ace Runner or Homer Unn? _____

  b. Who weighs more? _____

5. Whose batting average is lower, Steel N. Home or B. Ace Runner? _____

6a. Who lives in Nashville? _____

  b. What position does he play? _____

7a. Who plays right field? _____

  b. Where is he from? _____ c. How much does he weigh? _____

# Batting for Decimals

## Up at Bat: Working with Fractions and Decimals

### Learning Objective

Students find equivalent fractions, rename fractions in lowest terms, and convert fractions into decimals.

### What You'll Need

Batting for Decimals reproducible (page 32)
Trade Math Cards reproducible (page 29)
pencil and paper

### Directions

**1.** Before getting started, review with students the relationship between fractions and decimals. Also review renaming fractions in lowest terms and finding equivalent fractions.

**2.** Hand out copies of the Batting for Decimals reproducible and the Trade Math Cards reproducible and tell students that in this activity they will be working with fractions to find batting averages for baseball players. Explain to students that when a batting average is computed, an average of hits out of 1,000 is used. That doesn't mean that they wait until a baseball player goes to bat 1,000 times before computing the batting average. Instead, equivalent fractions are used and an average is estimated, based on how many times a player goes to bat and how many hits he gets. Although the big leagues use calculators, encourage students to do the math using equivalent fractions and their knowledge of decimals. Review the example on the reproducible with students to demonstrate the steps they will need to follow to calculate batting averages.

### Extension Activity

• Batting averages and other statistics are often found in newspapers and magazines during baseball season. Provide students with copies of the newspaper and have them track a particular player's batting average from week to week and convert the averages into fractions. Ask them to use the batting averages to try and predict how many hits that player will get in a game, a week, or a month.

### Answers

| | |
|---|---|
| 1a. Steel N. Home   282/1000 | 3a. 141 |
|     Izzy Saif   275/1000 | 3b. 70.5 |
|     B. Ace Runner   288/1000 | 4a. 644 |
|     Sammy Slugger   322/1000 | 4b. 32.2 |
|     Homer Unn   313/1000 | 4c. ~~16.4~~ 16.1 |
| 1b. 282/1000 = 141/500 | **All-Star Math** |
|     275/1000 = 11/40 | 5a. 28 |
|     288/1000 = 36/125 | 5b. 70 |
|     322/1000 = 161/500 | 5c. .280 |
| 2. 275 | |

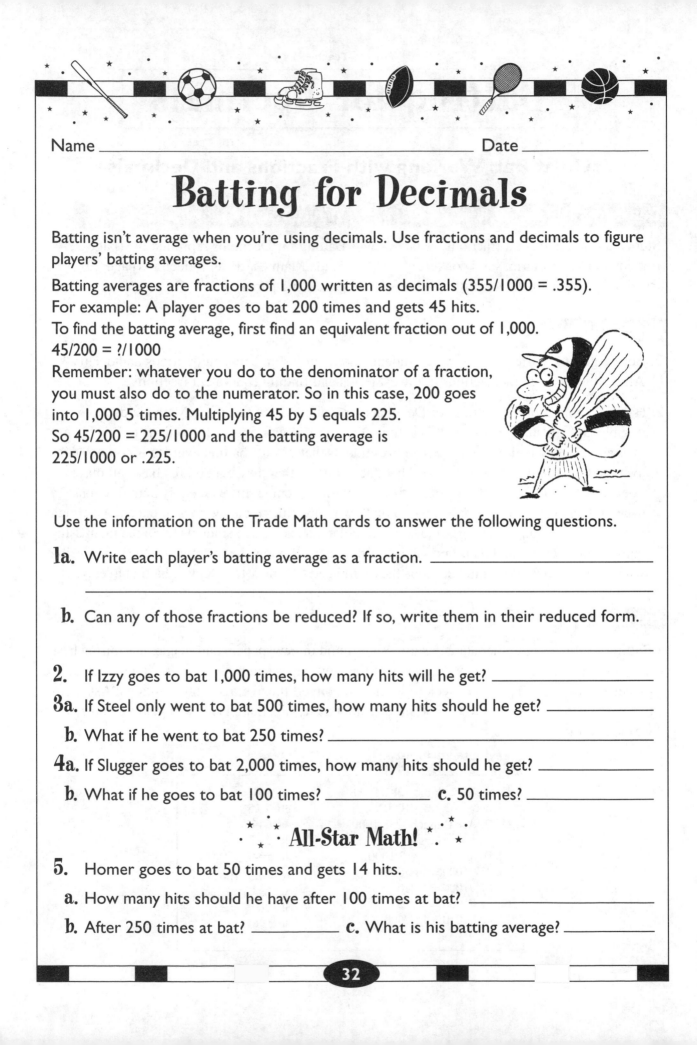

# Batting for Decimals

Batting isn't average when you're using decimals. Use fractions and decimals to figure players' batting averages.

Batting averages are fractions of 1,000 written as decimals (355/1000 = .355).
For example: A player goes to bat 200 times and gets 45 hits.
To find the batting average, first find an equivalent fraction out of 1,000.
45/200 = ?/1000
Remember: whatever you do to the denominator of a fraction, you must also do to the numerator. So in this case, 200 goes into 1,000 5 times. Multiplying 45 by 5 equals 225.
So 45/200 = 225/1000 and the batting average is 225/1000 or .225.

Use the information on the Trade Math cards to answer the following questions.

**1a.** Write each player's batting average as a fraction. _____

_____

**b.** Can any of those fractions be reduced? If so, write them in their reduced form.

_____

**2.** If Izzy goes to bat 1,000 times, how many hits will he get? _____

**3a.** If Steel only went to bat 500 times, how many hits should he get? _____

**b.** What if he went to bat 250 times? _____

**4a.** If Slugger goes to bat 2,000 times, how many hits should he get? _____

**b.** What if he goes to bat 100 times? _____ **c.** 50 times? _____

### ⋆ ⋆ All-Star Math! ⋆ ⋆

**5.** Homer goes to bat 50 times and gets 14 hits.

**a.** How many hits should he have after 100 times at bat? _____

**b.** After 250 times at bat? _____ **c.** What is his batting average? _____

# M(ath) TV

## Students tune in to sports and score big with math!

### Learning Objective

Students identify the different types of math skills used during sporting events.

### What You'll Need

television
pencil and paper

### Directions

1. Arrange for the class to watch a sporting event on television during class time. With the number of cable sports channels available today, there should be plenty to choose from at virtually any time of day. If not, arrange to have an event videotaped.

2. Before watching the event, brainstorm as a class a checklist of math skills. The list might include computation, measurement, fractions, decimals, and more. Students can refer to the checklist throughout the game but emphasize that the checklist is only a starting point. Students should add their own categories, as well. Also, the categories given can be further divided. Computation, for example, could be divided into addition, subtraction, etc.

3. Divide the class into teams of three or four, and challenge them to come up with examples of the mathematical skills that are used in the sporting event.

4. Once the skills have been identified, students should write one (or more) math problem to illustrate each individual skill. For example, if they are watching football, they could list "measurement" as a general skill and then write a problem that involves calculating yards and feet a player has run.

5. The point of this exercise is awareness and creativity. Students should work to develop their ability to not only identify information, but manipulate it as well.

### Extension Activity

• Although no one wants to encourage too much TV viewing, M(ath) TV can be great for vacation or weekend homework assignments. If students are going to spend some of their time away from school in front of a television, the time can be spent increasing their own awareness of the endless amount of math that is around them in their daily lives.

### Answers

Students' answers will vary.

# Basketball 1:
# Free-Throw Fractions

## Students hoop it up with a court full of fractions

### Learning Objective

Students use fractions to show how many shots basketball players make and miss. Use this activity with Free-Throw Percents and Free-Throw Decimals to show students the correlation between fractions, decimals, percents, and graphing.

### What You'll Need

Free-Throw Fractions reproducible (page 35)
pencil
calculator (optional)

### Directions

1. Hand out copies of Free-Throw Fractions. Remind students that a fraction represents a part of a whole. In this activity, the whole is the total number of free throws taken, and the part is either how many free throws were made or how many were missed.

2. Explain to students that as they work on each problem they should first write the fraction and then make sure it is in lowest terms.

3. For the All-Star Math, remind students that a fraction can be made into a decimal by dividing the numerator by the denominator. Students may use calculators for this part of the activity.

### Extension Activity

• Take the class to the playground or the gym for some exercise and some math! Divide the class into pairs. Have them alternate taking shots and keeping track of the shots they make and miss, and then write fractions based on the total number of shots taken.

### Answers

| | |
|---|---|
| 1a. $^2/_5$ | **All-Star Math** |
| 1b. $^3/_5$ | 1a. .4 |
| 2a. $^2/_5$ | 1b. .6 |
| 2b. $^3/_5$ | 2a. .4 |
| 3a. The fraction of shots that | 2b. .6 |
| he made is greater. | 3c. .54 |
| 3b. 28 | |
| 3c. $^7/_{13}$ | |

Name _____  Date _____

# Free-Throw Fractions

Hoops, Shooter, and Dunk'n are practicing their free throws. How
are they doing? To find the free-throw fractions for our players, place
the number of free throws made or missed over the number of free throws
attempted. Remember to reduce your fractions!

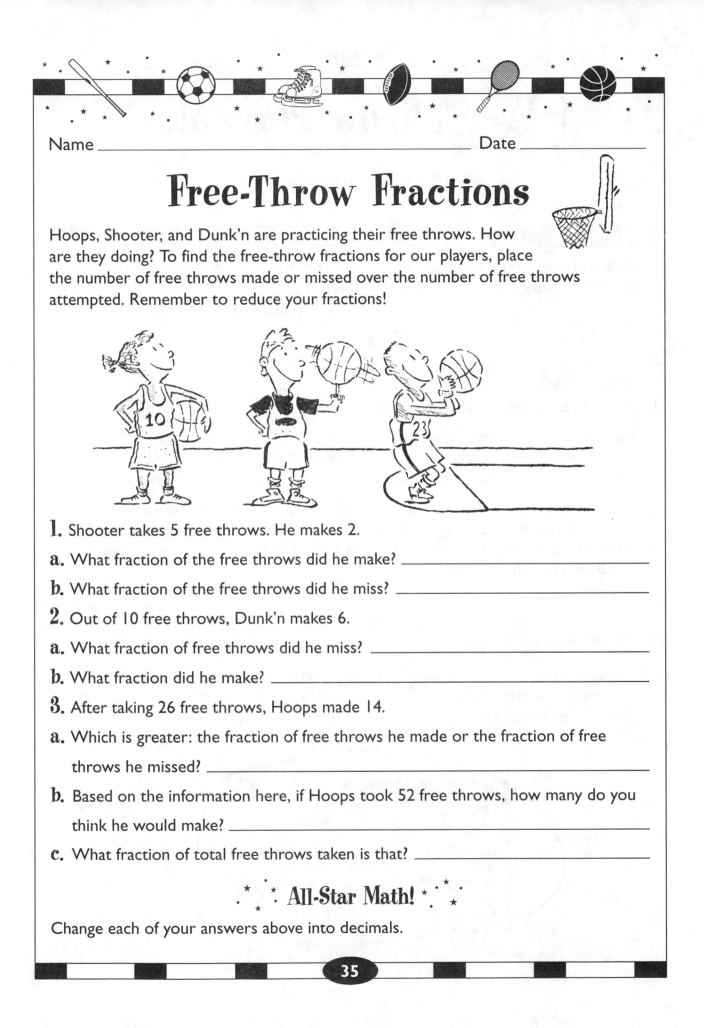

**1.** Shooter takes 5 free throws. He makes 2.

**a.** What fraction of the free throws did he make? _____

**b.** What fraction of the free throws did he miss? _____

**2.** Out of 10 free throws, Dunk'n makes 6.

**a.** What fraction of free throws did he miss? _____

**b.** What fraction did he make? _____

**3.** After taking 26 free throws, Hoops made 14.

**a.** Which is greater: the fraction of free throws he made or the fraction of free

throws he missed? _____

**b.** Based on the information here, if Hoops took 52 free throws, how many do you

think he would make? _____

**c.** What fraction of total free throws taken is that? _____

## ⋅ ⋆ ⋅ All-Star Math! ⋆ ⋅ ⋆

Change each of your answers above into decimals.

35

# Basketball 2:
# Free-Throw Percents

## More courtside calculating!

### Learning Objective

Students find equivalent fractions and then convert fractions into percents.

### What You'll Need

Free-Throw Percents reproducible (page 37)
pencil
calculator (optional)

### Directions

**1.** Review fractions with students and remind them that a percent is a fraction of 100.

**2.** Hand out copies of the Free-Throw Percents reproducible and tell students that in this activity they will be changing fractions into percents using equivalent fractions. First they will convert the fractions into fractions of 100 and then write the fraction as a percent.

**3.** As an alternative, you might have students change the fractions in these problems into decimals before changing them into percents. Students can use calculators for this part of the activity. Remind students that when changing a decimal to a percent, the decimal point is moved two places to the right.

### Extension Activity

• Percentages are everywhere: not only in the sports section of the newspaper, but on milk cartons, price tags, food labels, and more. Have students bring in everyday examples of percentages to class. Then work together to convert the percents to decimals and fractions.

### Answers

| | |
|---|---|
| 1. 40% | 3c. 65% |
| 2a. $3/4 = 75/100$ | 3d. 35% |
| 2b. $1/4 = 25/100$ | **All-Star Math** |
| 2c. 75% | 4a. $3/5$ |
| 2d. 25% | 4b. 6 |
| 3a. $13/20$ | 4c. 9 |
| 3b. $7/20$ | 4d. 120 |

# Free-Throw Percents

Hoops, Dunk'n, and Shooter are on the court again! How do their numbers add up? Follow the steps below to make sense of their percents.

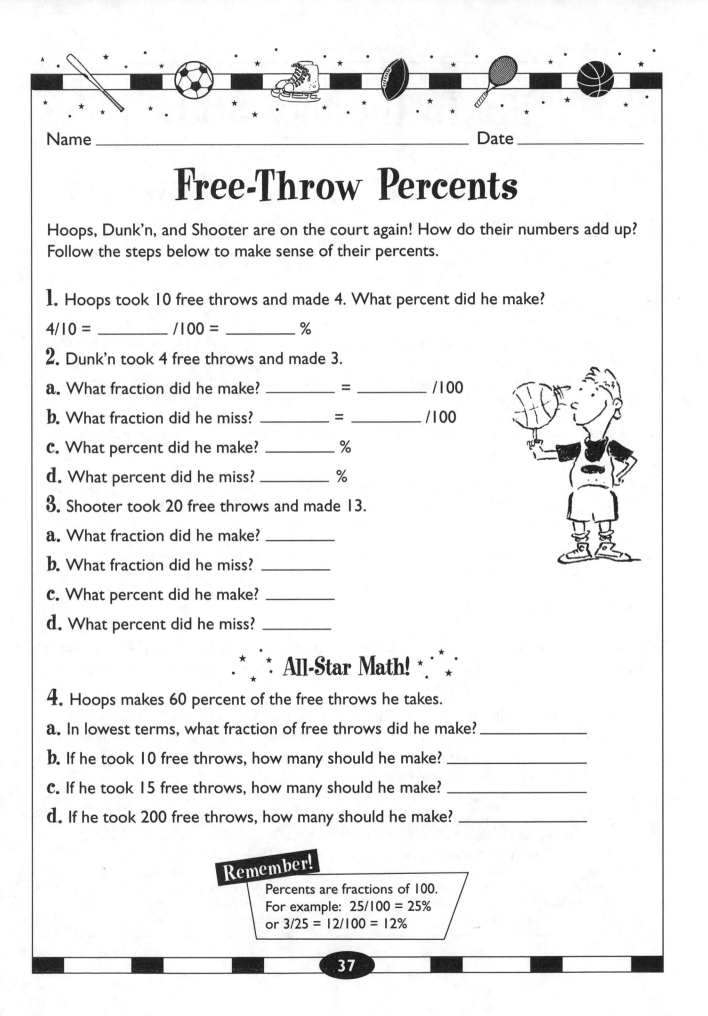

**1.** Hoops took 10 free throws and made 4. What percent did he make?

4/10 = _____ /100 = _____ %

**2.** Dunk'n took 4 free throws and made 3.

**a.** What fraction did he make? _____ = _____ /100

**b.** What fraction did he miss? _____ = _____ /100

**c.** What percent did he make? _____ %

**d.** What percent did he miss? _____ %

**3.** Shooter took 20 free throws and made 13.

**a.** What fraction did he make? _____

**b.** What fraction did he miss? _____

**c.** What percent did he make? _____

**d.** What percent did he miss? _____

## ⋅ ⋅ All-Star Math! ⋅ ⋅

**4.** Hoops makes 60 percent of the free throws he takes.

**a.** In lowest terms, what fraction of free throws did he make? _____

**b.** If he took 10 free throws, how many should he make? _____

**c.** If he took 15 free throws, how many should he make? _____

**d.** If he took 200 free throws, how many should he make? _____

**Remember!**

Percents are fractions of 100.
For example:  25/100 = 25%
or 3/25 = 12/100 = 12%

# Basketball 3:
# Pie in the Sky Stats

## Learning Objective

Students create pie graphs with fractions.

## What You'll Need

Pie in the Sky Stats reproducible (page 39)
pencil
colored pencils, crayons, or markers

## Directions

1. Explain to students that a graph is a picture representation of statistical information. Review some of the different types of graphs with students, including line graphs, bar graphs, pictographs, and pie graphs. Tell students that in this activity they will be creating pie graphs that represent fractions.

2. To begin, students need to write fractions that represent the number of baskets made and the number of baskets missed.

3. Next, students should color in the pie graph accordingly. The number of "pieces" they divide each pie into represents the total number of shots taken. Then they should color in the section of shots made one color and shots missed another color.

4. Remind students to clearly label which colors represent shots made and shots missed.

## Extension Activities

• Information from any of the activities that use fractions or percents can be used for a graphing activity. For example, students might create pie charts from the answers to the Free-Throw Fractions reproducible (page 35).

• To provide students with additional practice reading and working with graphs, find examples of graphs in newspapers and magazines to share in class or post on a bulletin board. *USA Today* is an excellent source of graphs. You can use the graphs as a lead-in to a wide variety of classroom discussions or as writing prompts.

## Answers

Graphs should reflect the following information:
Free throws: $3/4$ made, $1/4$ missed
3-point shots: $2/5$ made, $3/5$ missed
2-point shots: $4/7$ made, $3/7$ missed
Dunks: $3/5$ made, $2/5$ missed

**All-Star Math**
Students can use a bar graph to show the percentage of each different shot made. Students will need to convert the fractions into percentages before creating this graph.

# Pie in the Sky Stats

What fraction of each shot did our team make? Help Coach with his charts by coloring in the pies. Choose two different colors: one to represent shots made and another to represent shots missed.

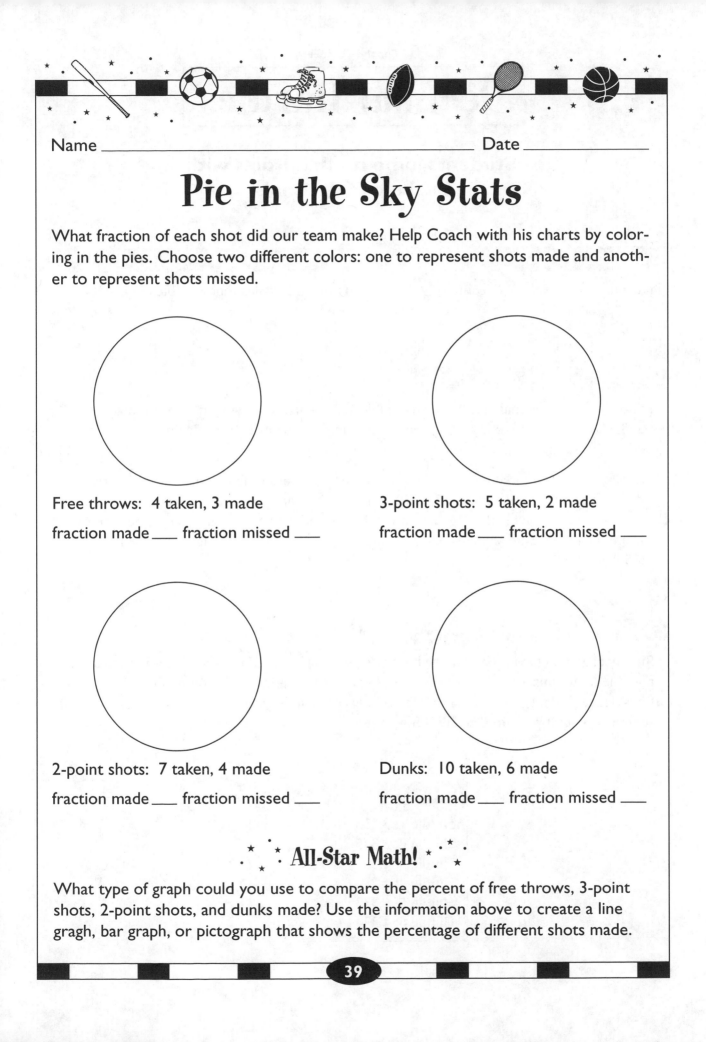

Free throws: 4 taken, 3 made

fraction made ___ fraction missed ___

3-point shots: 5 taken, 2 made

fraction made ___ fraction missed ___

2-point shots: 7 taken, 4 made

fraction made ___ fraction missed ___

Dunks: 10 taken, 6 made

fraction made ___ fraction missed ___

## ⋆ ⋆ All-Star Math! ⋆ ⋆

What type of graph could you use to compare the percent of free throws, 3-point shots, 2-point shots, and dunks made? Use the information above to create a line gragh, bar graph, or pictograph that shows the percentage of different shots made.

# Decimal Hurdles

## Students jump math hurdles with the help of decimals!

### Learning Objective

Students add and subtract decimals.

### What You'll Need

Decimal Hurdles reproducible (page 41)
pencil

### Directions

1. Distribute the Decimal Hurdles reproducible to students. Review with the class place value and adding and subtracting using decimals. Remind students to align decimal points before adding or subtracting.

2. Explain to students that they should start with the number printed on the hurdler's jersey and then add or subtract decimals with each hurdle. After each math hurdle, students should write their answer on the blank to the left of that hurdle and then add or subtract the next hurdle from that number. So students begin by adding .25 to 3.275. At hurdle 2, they will subtract .15 from 3.525.

### Extension Activity

• Simply changing the number on the hurdler's jersey or the numbers on the hurdles makes it possible to use this activity over and over. For an extra challenge, use more difficult computations. Have students multiply or divide decimals or include all four operations—addition, subtraction, multiplication, and division.

### Answers

Hurdle 1: 3.525
Hurdle 2: 3.375
Hurdle 3: 4.831
Hurdle 4: 4.28
Hurdle 5: 6.333
Hurdle 6: 4.334

# Decimal Hurdles

Help our math star Myrtle Hurdle clear her jumps and stay on track. Start with the number on our hurdler's jersey. Then add or subtract the decimal number on each hurdle as she moves around the course. Be sure to add or subtract the number on each hurdle from your new total.

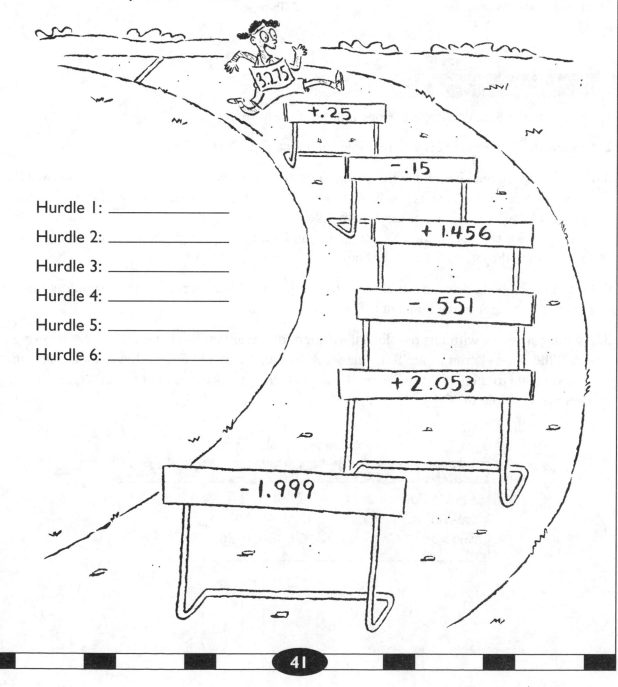

Hurdle 1: _____

Hurdle 2: _____

Hurdle 3: _____

Hurdle 4: _____

Hurdle 5: _____

Hurdle 6: _____

# Math's Slippery Slope

## Students can figure "multiple" ways to go when they ski the math slalom!

### Learning Objective

Students identify factors and multiples for specific numbers.

### What You'll Need

Math's Slippery Slope reproducible (page 43)
pencil

### Directions

1. Distribute the Math's Slippery Slope reproducible to students.

2. Review the difference between multiples and factors with students.

3. Explain to students that they will be using multiples and factors to guide the skiers down the slope. The number on each skier's bib must be either a multiple or a factor of the numbers printed on the flags on his or her course. Each skier must go down a different course. It may be helpful for students to first list all factors and multiples of each skier's number before trying to locate those numbers on the course.

4. Once they have discovered which skier travels down which course, students should write the name of that skier in the blank at the bottom of that run.

5. As students work with this problem, they might discover that Slick, number 4, could also go down the same ski run as Ice-Ski, number 8. But Ice-Ski could not go down Slick's ski run. Ask students to think about why this is true. Is there any factor or multiple of 8 that is not a factor or multiple of 4?

### Answers

Slick's Course: 2, 24, 16, 52, 84, 132
Ice-Ski's Course: 2, 96, 64, 72, 48, 56
Snow Joe's Course: 4, 84, 60, 120, 6, 36

# Math's Slippery Slope

Slick, Ice-Ski, and Snow Joe are in a race to the finish. To get to the bottom of the slope, each skier must take a different run. To find the correct path, the number on each skier's bib must be either a multiple or a factor of all the flag numbers on the path. Write the skier's name at the bottom of the path he or she should take.

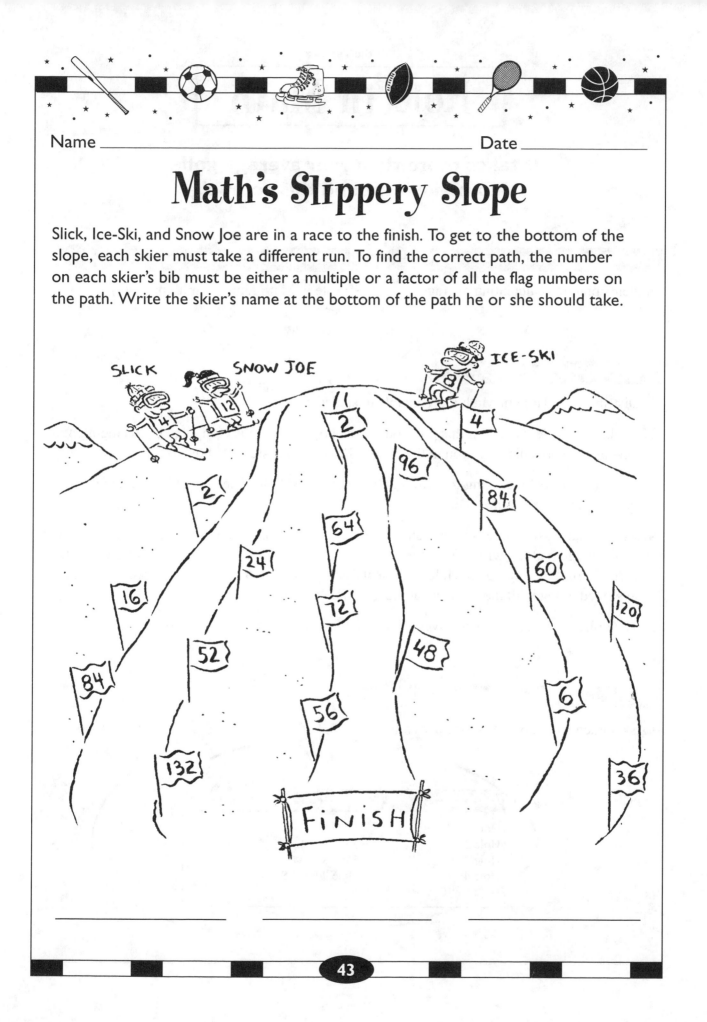

# Hole in Math

## It takes more than your average golfer to make it around this course!

### Learning Objective

Students practice calculating averages.

### What You'll Need

Hole in Math reproducible (page 45)
pencil

### Directions

**1.** Distribute the Hole in Math reproducible to students.

**2.** Explain to students that on this golf course, the golfer's score is computed by averaging numbers as he works his way around the course. Review with students how to find an average.

**3.** Students start by averaging the two numbers at the first hole. They should write that number on the blank next to the hole.

**4.** At each successive hole, students should take the average that they found at the previous hole and average it along with the numbers at that hole. For example, the average for the first hole is 5. To find the average at Hole 2, students should average 5 and 7. The answer (6) is then averaged along with the numbers at the next hole and so on.

**5.** The golfer's final score is the average after all 9 holes.

### Extension Activity

• Ask students to play the course backward, as well. Is the result different? Why or why not?

### Answers

| | |
|---|---|
| Hole 1: 5 | Hole 6: 12 |
| Hole 2: 6 | Hole 7: 11 |
| Hole 3: 9 | Hole 8: 13 |
| Hole 4: 7 | Hole 9/Final Score: 15 |
| Hole 5: 10 | |

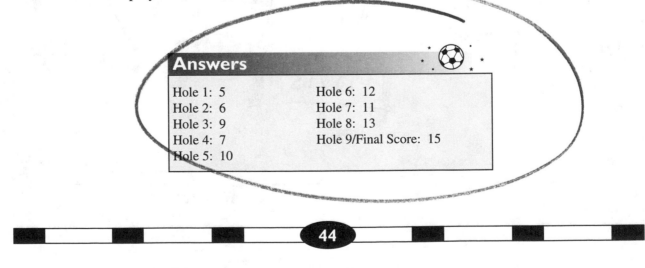

# Hole in Math

Move around this golf course by averaging the numbers along the way. Find the average of the two numbers at the first hole and write it on the blank. Then average the number you found at the first hole along with the number at the second hole and write down that answer. Average in the number found at the second hole with the numbers at the third hole. Keep going until you reach the end of the course.

4, 6 = ___

___, 7 = ___

___, 12 = ___

___, 8, 4 = ___

___, 9, 10, 14 = ___

___, 13, 13, ___ = ___

___, 10, 9, 7, 17 = ___

___, 25, 20, 10, 5, 7 = ___

___, 21, 22, 13, 8, 17, 11 = ___

Final Score: [ ]

# Math's Got It Covered

## How much ground do these soccer players have to cover? Math holds the answer!

### Learning Objective

Students calculate the area and perimeter of a field.

### What You'll Need

Math's Got It Covered reproducible (page 47)
calculator (optional)

### Directions

**1.** Distribute the Math's Got It Covered reproducible to students.

**2.** Review the concepts of *area* and *perimeter* with students. Make sure they understand the components—length and width—that make up both.

**3.** Highlight the difference between area and perimeter. Tell students that if they were to walk around the edge of the soccer field, the distance they would walk is called the perimeter. But if they were to measure the size of a blanket that would perfectly cover the entire field, that number would be the area.

**4.** Also explain that area is measured in square units: square feet, square yards, square miles, etc. For example: If a carpet has an area of 4 square feet, that means that 4 squares, each 1 foot wide and 1 foot long, would perfectly cover the carpet. Refer students to the square-unit diagram on the reproducible for visual reinforcement of this idea.

### Extension Activity

• Divide students into small groups and take them outside or to the school gym. Using a tape measure, have each group figure out the perimeters and areas of various playing fields at your school.

### Answers

| | |
|---|---|
| 1a. 100 yards, 300 feet | 2b. 2,500 square yards, 22,500 square feet |
| 1b. 50 yards, 150 feet | 3a. 410 yards |
| 1c. 300 yards, 900 feet | 3b. 9,750 square yards |
| 1d. 5,000 square yards, 45,000 square feet | **All-Star Math** |
| 2a. 200 yards, 600 feet | Answers will vary. |

# Math's Got It Covered

These soccer players sure have a lot of ground to cover. Just how much exactly?
Look at the picture and answer the questions.

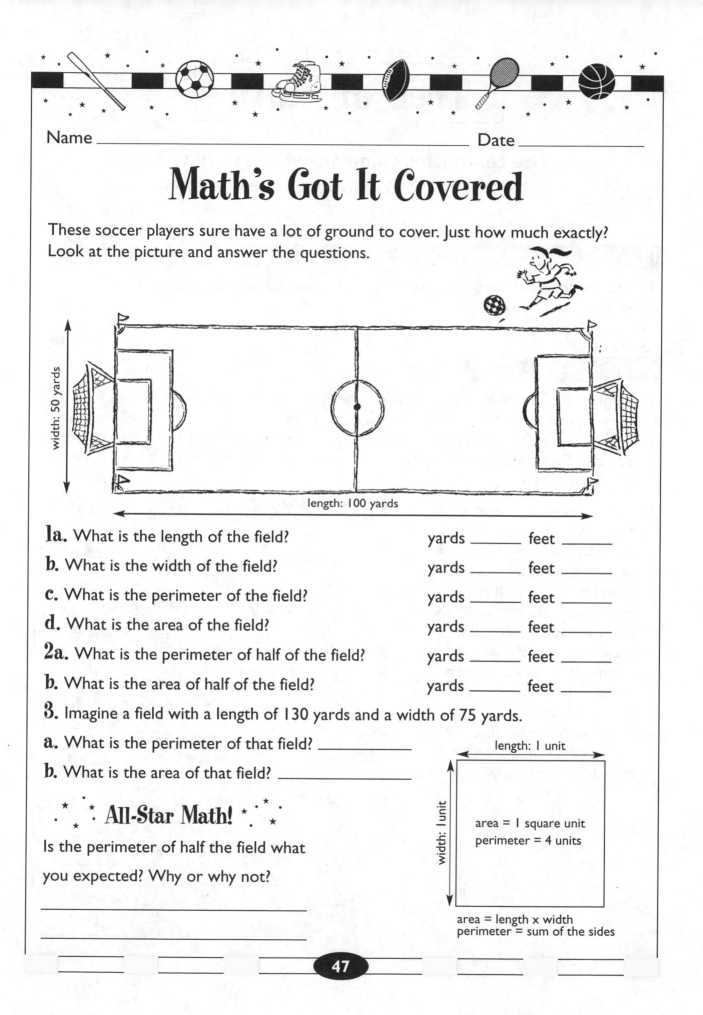

width: 50 yards

length: 100 yards

**1a.** What is the length of the field?      yards _____ feet _____

**b.** What is the width of the field?      yards _____ feet _____

**c.** What is the perimeter of the field?      yards _____ feet _____

**d.** What is the area of the field?      yards _____ feet _____

**2a.** What is the perimeter of half of the field?      yards _____ feet _____

**b.** What is the area of half of the field?      yards _____ feet _____

**3.** Imagine a field with a length of 130 yards and a width of 75 yards.

**a.** What is the perimeter of that field? _____

**b.** What is the area of that field? _____

## ⋆ ⋆ All-Star Math! ⋆ ⋆

Is the perimeter of half the field what

you expected? Why or why not?

_____

_____

length: 1 unit

width: 1 unit

area = 1 square unit
perimeter = 4 units

area = length x width
perimeter = sum of the sides

# Tree of Math

## The team isn't going anywhere until they get dressed. Combination trees can help!

### Learning Objective

Students use logic and computation skills to build a combination tree.

### What You'll Need

Tree of Math reproducible (page 49)
pencil

### Directions

**1.** Distribute the Tree of Math reproducible to the class. Review combination trees with students. Explain that combination trees are a visual way to calculate the number of combinations you can make from a set of objects. Students should work from left to right building their tree. Every item in each column should be connected to every item in the column or columns next to it.

**2.** Students should first connect the items of clothing, forming the "tree." After the connections have been made, the students should then add up all the possible clothing combinations and write the number in the blank to the left. Explain to students that they can also find the answer by multiplying the number of items in each column. For example, for the first problem students can multiply 2 x 3 x 4 to find the answer of 24.

### Answers

# Tree of Math

How many outfits can these players wear? Use combination trees to find out. To create a combination tree, connect every item in the first column to each item in the second column. Then connect every item in the second column to the items in the third column and so on. Count up all the connections and write the number of possible uniform combinations on the blanks to the left. We've started the first tree for you!

# Get the Angle on Pool

## Students size up shapes with some sharp shooters!

### Learning Objective

Students identify and draw polygons, and label acute, obtuse, and right angles.

### What You'll Need

Get the Angle on Pool reproducible (page 51)
colored pencils
ruler

### Directions

1. Distribute the Get the Angle on Pool reproducible to students. Review the different types of polygons and angles with students. Remind students that an acute angle measures between 0 and 90 degrees, an obtuse angle measures between 90 and 180 degrees, and a right angle measures exactly 90 degrees. Draw their attention to the Know Your Polygons! box on the reproducible.

2. Explain to students that for this activity they will be drawing as many polygons as they can on the pool table. The corners of the polygons should be formed by either the 6 pockets or the 12 diamond markings on the table. To get students started, share the sample below.

3. Students can use different colored pencils to distinguish between the different types of polygons and angles.

### Answers

Students' answers will vary. Check for accuracy.

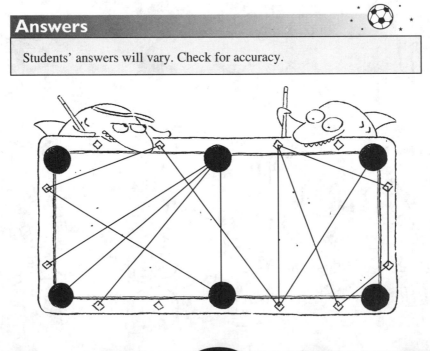

Name _____              Date _____

# Get the Angle on Pool

These pool sharks sure know their geometry. Do you? Use the 6 pockets and 12 diamonds on our pool table to draw as many different polygons as you can. Label acute, obtuse, and right angles.

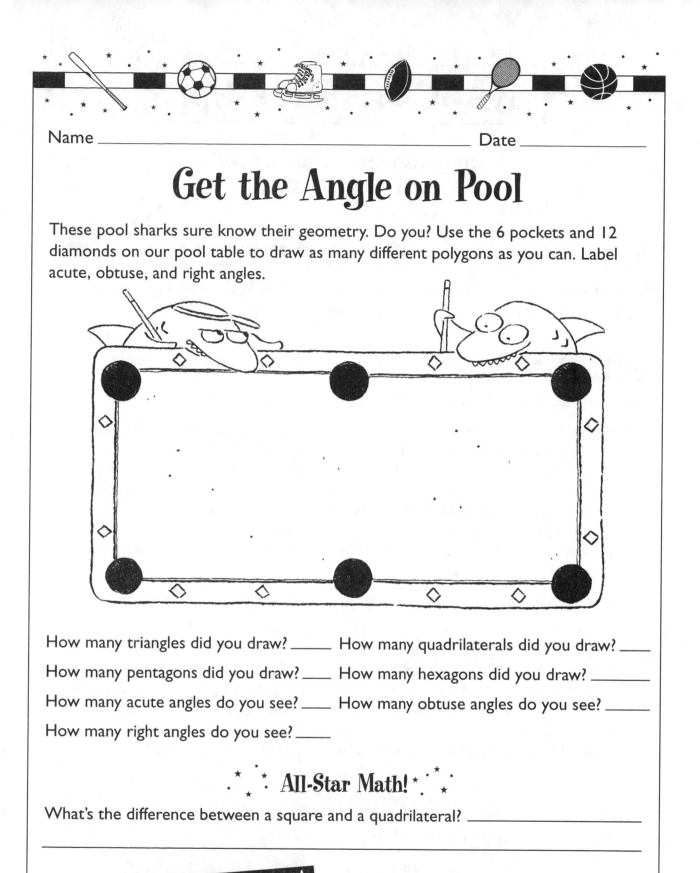

How many triangles did you draw? _____  How many quadrilaterals did you draw? _____

How many pentagons did you draw? _____  How many hexagons did you draw? _____

How many acute angles do you see? _____  How many obtuse angles do you see? _____

How many right angles do you see? _____

## ⋆ ⋅ ⋅ All-Star Math! ⋆ ⋅ ⋆

What's the difference between a square and a quadrilateral? _____

_____

**Know Your Polygons!**

triangle: three sides          quadrilateral: four sides
pentagon: five sides           hexagon: six sides

# NASCAR Adds Up!

## Students race for points with math and NASCAR.

### Learning Objective

Students use information from a chart to solve multistep problems.

### What You'll Need

NASCAR Adds Up! reproducible (page 53)
pencil and paper

### Directions

1. Distribute the NASCAR Adds Up! reproducible to the class.

2. Explain to students that in NASCAR racing, drivers earn points for each race based on their finishing position. The points earned for each race are added to a driver's overall total. So a driver who has earned 185 points in the first race and 170 points in the second race has a total of 355 points. In this activity, students will need to tabulate the total points each driver has earned after each race to answer the questions. They should refer to the chart to find the point values for each finishing position. To make the task easier, students might create a chart on the back of the reproducible that includes the points the drivers earn with each race and their new point total after each race.

3. Students should then use the point tabulations they've calculated to answer the questions.

### Extension Activity

• Have students track NASCAR results over several races and keep track of the points earned by different drivers. Different groups of students could be assigned to track the results of one or two particular drivers. Students can create a graph to present the results. This extension may also be easily combined with the extension activity for Math on Track (page 18).

### Answers

1. Slick Vick (345 pts.);
   Race Ace (332 pts.);
   Speedy Smith (330 pts.)
2. Slick Vick (690 pts.);
   Speedy Smith (655 pts.);
   Race Ace (616 pts.)
3. 825
4. 840
5. 786
6. Slick Vick

Name _____ Date _____

# NASCAR Adds Up!

Get the points? Our drivers do! Use math to find out how many. Read the results and add up the points. The driver with the most points after five races wins!

| Finishing Position | Points |
|---|---|
| 1 | 175 |
| 2 | 170 |
| 3 | 165 |
| 4 | 160 |
| 5 | 155 |
| 6 | 150 |
| 7 | 146 |
| 8 | 142 |
| 9 | 138 |
| 10 | 134 |

**Bonus Points**
5 points if the driver led the race at the end of at least one lap.
5 points if the driver led the race at the end of the most laps.

To find the score:
Finishing position points
+ bonus points
_____
race points

**Race Results**

Race #1
Speedy Smith: 3rd place, no bonus points
Race Ace: 8th place, 5 bonus points
Slick Vick, 2nd place, 5 bonus points

Race #2
Speedy Smith: 4th place, 5 bonus points
Race Ace: 1st place, 10 bonus points
Slick Vick: 3rd place, 5 bonus points

Race #3
Speedy Smith: 5th place, no bonus points
Race Ace: 7th place, no bonus points
Slick Vick: 4th place, no bonus points

Race #4
Speedy Smith: 3rd place, 5 bonus points
Race Ace: 9th place, no bonus points
Slick Vick: 1st place, 10 bonus points

Race #5
Speedy Smith: 2nd place, no bonus points
Race Ace: 3rd place, 5 bonus points
Slick Vick: 6th place, no bonus points

**1.** After two races who was in first, second, and third place? _____

_____

**2a.** After four races who was in first, second, and third place? _____

_____

**b.** What was the difference in points between first place and third place? _____

**3.** How many total points did Speedy earn? _____

**4.** How many total points did Slick Vick earn? _____

**5.** How many total points did Race Ace earn? _____

**6.** Of our three drivers, who is the overall winner after five races? _____

# Touchdown Math

## Students tackle some prealgebra with a gridiron full of math.

### Learning Objective

Students solve simple equations.

### What You'll Need

Touchdown Math reproducible (page 55)

### Directions

1. Distribute the Touchdown Math reproducible to the class.

2. Discuss with students the simple equations that appear on the reproducible. Explain that the letters in each problem are being used to represent different numbers. At the bottom of the reproducible they will find the number values for each letter. After they have substituted the numbers for the letters, they will have a basic computation problem that they should be able to solve. Students can use the back of the page for their calculations and write the answers on the front.

3. Draw their attention to the example problem on the reproducible and emphasize that a step-by-step approach breaks each problem down into very manageable parts.

### Extension Activities

• A safety is worth 2 points and so is a 2-point conversion. Have students create their own symbols for a safety and a two-point conversion. Then have them write a score using all of the symbols they've learned and give it to a classmate to figure out.

• Have students look up the results of football games in the newspaper and rewrite the scores as algebraic equations. Post their equations on a bulletin board and challenge students to solve their classmates' problems.

### Answers

| | | | |
|---|---|---|---|
| Razorback Hogs | 34 | Junebugs | 14 |
| Flying Squirrels | 22 | Vipers | 9 |
| Lady Lizards | 16 | Killer Bees | 30 |
| Freeport Frogs | 26 | Wildebeests | 26 |
| Porcupines | 55 | Crocodile Tears | 21 |
| Sea Urchins | 57 | Camel Humps | 27 |

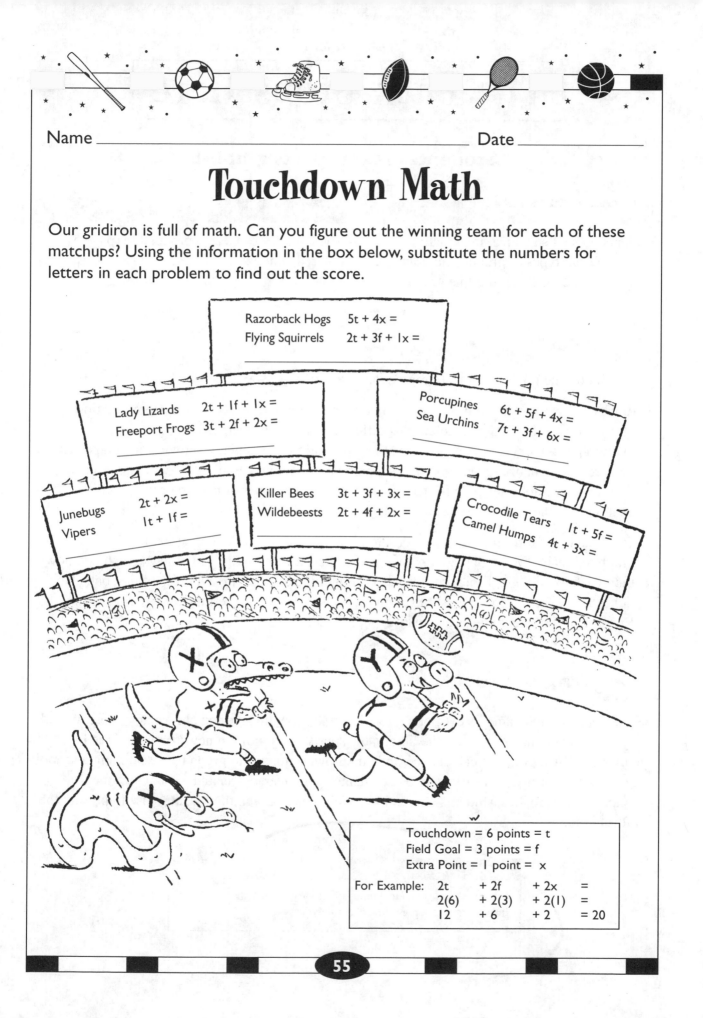

Our gridiron is full of math. Can you figure out the winning team for each of these matchups? Using the information in the box below, substitute the numbers for letters in each problem to find out the score.

Razorback Hogs    $5t + 4x =$
Flying Squirrels    $2t + 3f + 1x =$
_____

Lady Lizards    $2t + 1f + 1x =$
Freeport Frogs    $3t + 2f + 2x =$
_____

Porcupines    $6t + 5f + 4x =$
Sea Urchins    $7t + 3f + 6x =$
_____

Junebugs    $2t + 2x =$
Vipers    $1t + 1f =$
_____

Killer Bees    $3t + 3f + 3x =$
Wildebeests    $2t + 4f + 2x =$
_____

Crocodile Tears    $1t + 5f =$
Camel Humps    $4t + 3x =$
_____

Touchdown = 6 points = t
Field Goal = 3 points = f
Extra Point = 1 point = x

For Example:   $2t$   $+ 2f$   $+ 2x$   $=$
               $2(6)$   $+ 2(3)$   $+ 2(1)$   $=$
               $12$   $+ 6$   $+ 2$   $= 20$

Name _____    Date _____

# The Puck Stops Here

## Students create sports graphs!

### Learning Objective

Students present statistical information using different types of graphs, including bar graphs, pictographs, and line graphs.

### What You'll Need

The Puck Stops Here reproducible (page 57)
colored pencils

### Directions

1. Distribute The Puck Stops Here reproducible to students.

2. Review graphing with students and remind them that graphing is a visual representation of numerical information. Explain that different graphs—line graphs, bar graphs, or pictographs—work best depending on the information that is being shown. Line graphs are ideal to show changes over time. A bar graph is a useful way to directly compare information. A pictograph uses pictures to represent a certain number of people or things. Share examples of the different types of graphs with the class.

3. Tell students that for the first three problems on the reproducible, they are told which type of graph to create. For the last graph, they get to choose both the information to graph and how they wish to graph it. Topics for the graphs might include batting averages of baseball stars, ticket prices for different types of sporting events, or a team's record over a period of time. Encourage students to be as as creative as possible.

### Extension Activity

• Students can find examples of sports information that can be graphed almost anywhere, including in reference materials from the library, the sports section of the newspaper, and the local television news. Students can also compile their own statistics to graph by researching a school team's record or taking a survey among students about a sports-related topic. Once they've compiled the statistics, students can decide which type of graph they want to use to present the information.

### Answers

Students' styles and techniques will vary. Check that the information is represented accurately.

# The Puck Stops Here

Read these cool hockey stats and then graph the information. We've included the type of graph to use for each one.

**1.** Create a **pictograph** with these stats.

**Numbers of Stanley Cup Championships Won:**

| | |
|---|---|
| Montreal Canadiens | 24 |
| Toronto Maple Leafs | 13 |
| Detroit Red Wings | 8 |
| Boston Bruins | 5 |
| New York Rangers | 4 |

**2.** Create a **bar graph** with these stats.

**Stanley Cup Playoff Stats:**

| | Mark Messier | Wayne Gretzky |
|---|---|---|
| points | 295 | 382 |
| assists | 186 | 260 |
| goals | 122 | 109 |

**3.** Create a **line graph** with these stats.

**Franchise value of the Chicago Blackhawks, 1991–1996:**

| | |
|---|---|
| 1991 | $61 million |
| 1992 | $67 million |
| 1993 | $80 million |
| 1994 | $102 million |
| 1995 | $122 million |
| 1996 | $151 million |

**4.** Graph your stats! Compile sports statistics—from a favorite team or one of your school team's records—and then graph it on the back of this page. Which kind of graph did you decide to use, and why?

# "Weigh" Out Math

## Turn students into math heavyweights with this weighty activity.

### Learning Objective

Students practice multiplying with decimals as they convert kilograms to pounds.

### What You'll Need

"Weigh" Out Math reproducible (page 59)
pencil

### Directions

1. Distribute the "Weigh" Out Math reproducible to students.

2. This exercise uses several skills. Review converting weights, multiplying with decimals, and the metric system with students before beginning. A good understanding of each of these skills individually will make it much easier for students to use them together.

3. Explain to students that they should first convert all of the weights in kilograms to weights in pounds. Then they should answer the questions.

### Extension Activity

- As a math-history project, have students research ancient measures, such the Greek cubits and the Roman stadium. The *World Almanac* is one resource for this information. Students can then create math problems using this information.

### Answers

Weights in pounds are:

| | |
|---|---|
| Flyweight | 112.2 pounds |
| Bantamweight | 117.7 pounds |
| Featherweight | 125.4 pounds |
| Lightweight | 134.2 pounds |
| Welterweight | 146.3 pounds |
| Middleweight | 159.5 pounds |
| Light Heavyweight | 173.8 pounds |
| Heavyweight | 173.8+ pounds |

1. 159.5
2. 9.5
3a. Two flyweights weigh more.
3b. At least 23 kg or 50.6 lbs.

4a. 132.5 kg
4b. 64.9 lbs.
4c. 29.5 kg

**All Star Math**

| | |
|---|---|
| Flyweight | 51,000 grams/1,785 oz. |
| Bantamweight | 53,500 grams/1,872.5 oz. |
| Featherweight | 57,000 grams/1,992 oz. |
| Lightweight | 61,000 grams/2,135 oz. |
| Welterweight | 66,500 grams/2,327.5 oz. |
| Middleweight | 72,500 grams/2,537.5 oz. |
| Light Heavyweight | 79,000 grams/2,765 oz. |
| Heavyweight | 79,000+ grams/2,765+ oz. |

# "Weigh" Out Math

Our heavy hitters know how many kilos they're carrying, but pound per pound, they're stumped! Use the conversion chart below to convert each weight category from kilograms to pounds. Write each decimal out to the nearest tenth. Then answer the questions.

Conversion: 1 kilogram (kg) = 2.2 pounds (lbs.)

| Boxing Weight Categories | | |
|---|---|---|
| | Kilograms | Pounds |
| Flyweight | 51 kg | _____ lbs. |
| Bantamweight | 53.5 kg | _____ lbs. |
| Featherweight | 57 kg | _____ lbs. |
| Lightweight | 61 kg | _____ lbs. |
| Welterweight | 66.5 kg | _____ lbs. |
| Middleweight | 72.5 kg | _____ lbs. |
| Light Heavyweight | 79 kg | _____ lbs. |
| Heavyweight | 79 + kg | _____ lbs. |

1. How many pounds should a middleweight weigh? _____

2. How many more kilograms does a welterweight weigh than a featherweight? _____

3a. Which weighs more: two flyweights or one light heavyweight? _____

b. How much more? pounds _____ kilograms _____

4a. How many kilograms do a bantamweight and a light heavyweight weigh together? _____

b. How many fewer pounds is that than the combined weight of two 81-kilogram heavyweights? _____ c. How many fewer kilograms is that? _____

## ⋆ ⋅ ⋆ All-Star Math! ⋆ ⋅ ⋆

How many ounces would our fighters weigh? How many grams? Write your answers on the back of this page.

# Time Is on Your Side

## Students work around the clock timing rounds for sumo wrestling and other sports.

### Learning Objective

Students measure lengths of time on a clock.

### What You'll Need

Time Is on Your Side reproducible (page 61)
colored pencils or pens

### Directions

**1.** Distribute the Time Is on Your Side reproducible to the class. Explain to students that with this activity they will be measuring time using a clock face.

**2.** Go over the information with students. Point out that for some matches there is a minimum and maximum amount of time. For each sport, students should draw a solid line to represent a definite time and a dotted line to represent possible time. Students should begin at zero for each sport. See example below.

**3.** Instruct students to use different colored pencils so that it is easier to recognize the competition times of the different sports. Students can create a simple key by marking the color they used by the corresponding sport on the list at the bottom of the page.

**4.** Once students have completed their graphs, ask them if they have ever seen a graph like this before. What is helpful about this type of graph? What other kind of graph could they draw to present the same information?

### Extension Activity

• Have students map how they spend an hour of their time. For example: Students could map how much time they spend brushing their teeth, taking a shower, getting dressed, eating breakfast, and traveling to school. After-school activities—including homework!—could also be mapped.

### Answers

Check students' work to ensure the information is represented accurately.

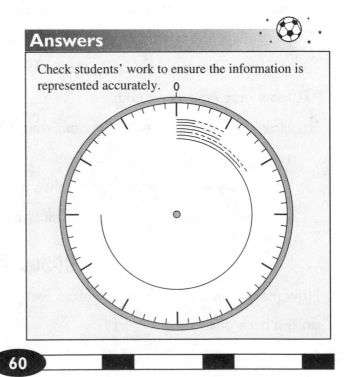

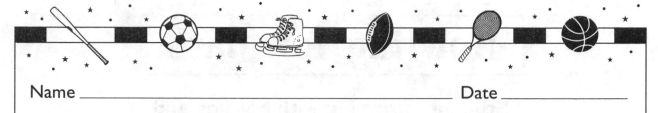

# Time Is on Your Side

Mark the length of time each competition takes on the clock. Start at 0 and use solid lines to represent definite time and dotted lines to represent possible time. Use a different color for each sport. Make a key for your chart by marking the color you used by corresponding sport on the list below.

For example: If a match usually lasts a minimum of 2 minutes and a maximum of 5 minutes, draw a solid line from 0 to 2 minutes and a dotted line from 2 to 5 minutes. We did this one for you. Now you can do the rest!

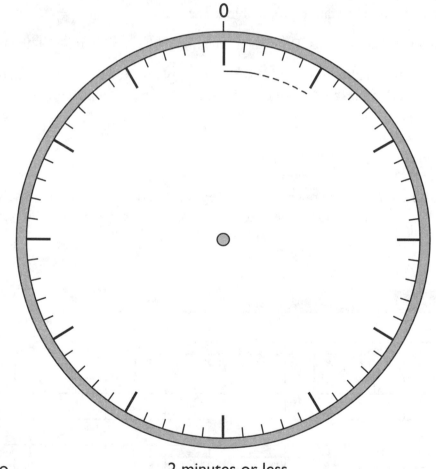

| Sumo | 2 minutes or less |
| Karate | minimum 3 minutes, maximum 5 minutes |
| Fencing | 6 minutes |
| Judo | minimum 2 minutes, maximum 10 minutes |
| Greco-Roman Wrestling | 3 rounds, 3 minutes each |
| Professional Boxing | 15 rounds, 3 minutes each |

# Bowling for Math

## Students score big with bowling and math that's right up their alley!

### Learning Objective

Students practice basic computation skills as they tabulate bowling scores.

### What You'll Need

Bowling for Math reproducible (page 63)
pencil

### Directions

**1.** Distribute the Bowling for Math reproducible to the class.

**2.** Go over scoring with the students. Draw their attention to the scoring rules on the reproducible.

**3.** Be sure to review the method for scoring strikes and spares. Remind students that a "/" represents a spare, an "X" represents a strike, and " – " represents no pins being knocked down.

### Extension Activity

• Go bowling! Give students the opportunity to keep score and do the math themselves. Be careful: Many bowling alleys now have automatic scoring. Ask the attendant to turn it off, if possible.

### Answers

**Bo Lin Score Sheet**

| frame 1 | | frame 2 | | frame 3 | | frame 4 | | frame 5 | | frame 6 | | frame 7 | | frame 8 | | frame 9 | | frame 10 | | |
|---|---|---|---|---|---|---|---|---|---|---|---|---|---|---|---|---|---|---|---|---|
| 2 | 5 | 4 | 3 | 2 | / | 9 | – | 6 | 2 | X | | 7 | 1 | – | / | 4 | 5 | 6 | / | 9 |
| 7 | | 14 | | 33 | | 42 | | 50 | | 68 | | 76 | | 90 | | 99 | | 118 | | |

**Striker Smith Score Sheet**

| frame 1 | | frame 2 | | frame 3 | | frame 4 | | frame 5 | | frame 6 | | frame 7 | | frame 8 | | frame 9 | | frame 10 | | |
|---|---|---|---|---|---|---|---|---|---|---|---|---|---|---|---|---|---|---|---|---|
| 3 | 5 | 5 | – | X | | 7 | 2 | 6 | 3 | 2 | / | 8 | 1 | 7 | / | X | | 6 | 3 | – |
| 8 | | 13 | | 32 | | 41 | | 50 | | 68 | | 77 | | 97 | | 116 | | 125 | | |

# Bowling for Math

Who will win the big bowling matchup? Add up these bowlers' scores to find out. Here's how bowling games are scored:

**1.** Each game is divided into 10 frames. In each frame, bowlers get two chances to knock down all 10 pins. Look at Ally Katz's score in frame 1: The number of pins knocked down are written in the smaller boxes above (3, 4). Their total is written beneath (7). In frame 2 she knocked down 6 pins on her first try, then the rest on her second. When all the pins are knocked down on the second try, it is called a spare. A spare is represented by "/". The score for a spare is 10 points plus the number of pins knocked down on the next try. To find the score in frame 2, Ally waited until she rolled the first ball in frame 3. Then she added 7 (score in frame 1) + 10 (points for the spare) + 4 (points for the first try after the spare). So her score for frame 2 is 21.

**2.** In frame 4, Ally knocked down all 10 pins on her first try. That's called a strike, and it's represented by "X". A strike is worth 10 points plus the number of pins knocked down on the next two tries. If no pins are knocked down, a "–" is marked in the box.

**3.** Frame 10 has three boxes. If you score a strike or a spare in the first two rolls of frame 10, you get an extra roll. To find the score for frame 10, add up all the pins that were knocked down and add them to the score in frame 9. Ally Katz scored 20 points in frame 10 because she bowled a spare (6 + 4) and a strike (10). Her final score was 117 + 20, or 137.

Ally Katz Score Sheet

| frame 1 | | frame 2 | | frame 3 | | frame 4 | | frame 5 | | frame 6 | | frame 7 | | frame 8 | | frame 9 | | frame 10 | | |
|---|---|---|---|---|---|---|---|---|---|---|---|---|---|---|---|---|---|---|---|---|
| 3 | 4 | 6 | / | 4 | 2 | X | | 7 | 2 | X | | 8 | / | 6 | – | X | | 6 | / | X |
| | 7 | | 21 | | 27 | | 46 | | 55 | | 75 | | 91 | | 97 | | 117 | | | 137 |

Bo Lin Score Sheet

| frame 1 | | frame 2 | | frame 3 | | frame 4 | | frame 5 | | frame 6 | | frame 7 | | frame 8 | | frame 9 | | frame 10 | | |
|---|---|---|---|---|---|---|---|---|---|---|---|---|---|---|---|---|---|---|---|---|
| 2 | 5 | 4 | 3 | 2 | / | 9 | – | 6 | 2 | X | | 7 | 1 | – | / | 4 | 5 | 6 | / | 9 |
| | | | | | | | | | | | | | | | | | | | | |

Striker Smith Score Sheet

| frame 1 | | frame 2 | | frame 3 | | frame 4 | | frame 5 | | frame 6 | | frame 7 | | frame 8 | | frame 9 | | frame 10 | | |
|---|---|---|---|---|---|---|---|---|---|---|---|---|---|---|---|---|---|---|---|---|
| 3 | 5 | 5 | – | X | | 7 | 2 | 6 | 3 | 2 | / | 8 | 1 | 7 | / | X | | 6 | 3 | – |
| | | | | | | | | | | | | | | | | | | | | |

# Swingin' Division

## Students go head to head as they take a swing at dividing with remainders

### Learning Objective

Students divide 2- and 3-digit numbers with remainders.

### What You'll Need

chalkboard and chalk

### Directions

**1.** Divide the class into two teams.

**2.** Explain to students that the game is played like baseball, with three bases and a home plate.

**3.** The team at bat decides on a number with at least three digits and sends a batter to the plate. The batter announces the number. The opposing team then pitches a smaller number to the batter. The team at bat must divide its number by the number that was pitched to them and give the answer with a remainder. Have students complete their work on the chalkboard. If they give the correct answer, they advance one base. If they give an incorrect answer, the batter is out. After three outs, the sides change.

**4.** A team can score a "home run" if the opposing team pitches a number that divides evenly into its number with no remainder.

**5.** For every "run," a point is scored. The game is over after 9 innings. If the score is tied, then go into extra innings.

**6.** For shorter class periods, play with fewer innings or fewer outs.

### Extension Activity

• This game can be used for a wide variety of operations and is a fun way to review a particular skill before a test.

### Answers

Every game will provide different answers.